ABOUT THE BOOK

This book is both a memoir and a devotional. I'm not a writer, but God told me to write this. In obedience to the Lord, I gratefully share how He has worked in my life and the miracles He has shown me. I still get excited when I read the miracles, and I am so thankful for what He has shown me.

The Miracles In My Life

Sheila Shelton

*To Brenda with much love,
Sheila Shelton*

Registration Number
TXu 1-847-124
Effective date of registration:
September 25, 2012

Copyright © 2013 Sheila Shelton
All rights reserved.

ISBN: 1-4810-1344-0
ISBN-13: 9781481013444

ACKNOWLEDGEMENT

I would like to thank Alexandra Clair, author of <u>*WOOD'S END*</u>, for assisting with the editing of this book. Her website is www.alexandraclair.com.

To listen to Alex interviewing me on internel radio, you can go to www.blogtalkradio.com/chrisianfreedom/2013/04/13/the-unseen-world. She interviewed me on the second half of the show.

FOREWORD

As I look back now, I can see how the Lord worked in my life. He always took good care of my autistic, non-verbal, forty years old son, Dale Wilson and me. I learned to depend on Jesus Christ, but life sure was hard.

The Bible tells us: **In all your ways acknowledge Him, and He will make your paths straight (Proverbs 3: 6).** I have learned to get on my knees before I do anything or go anywhere. It's amazing how this has helped Dale and me.

The Lord has shown me so many things, but I didn't always understand what He was trying to show me. **We see now in a cloudy mirror. For now we see in a mirror dimly, but then face to face; no I know in part, but then I will know fully just as I also have been fully known (1st Corinthians 13: 12).** I just know that I will trust in the Lord with all my heart, and believe His word, even when I don't understand.

Other things have happened that have not been included in these pages, more personal things that I did not feel at liberty to reveal. I'm not a writer, but the Lord told to write these experiences down. Then I read: **Publish His glorious deeds among the nations. Tell everyone the amazing things He does (1st Chronicles 16:24).**

If I had lived a life closer to the Lord, Jesus, I don't know if all these things would have happened, but then again, the Lord might have used this opportunity to draw me near to Him so that He could show me the events of life that I call my miracles, and what is truly important about life. I can say, as many of you can, that His power is awesome!

My sins have been great, but I called upon the only One who could save and forgive me, and that is Jesus Christ. **For by grace you have been saved through faith; and that not of yourselves, it is the gift of God; not as a result of works, so that no one may boast (Ephesians 2: 8, 9).** I'm not perfect, just forgiven and this frees me to worship Christ with a grateful heart.

I have failed many times and been judged harshly by other believers, but who is the worse, the sinner or the one who judges? I wouldn't go back and take away anything that God has taught me, even though much of what I learned came from pain. Scripture tells us how to be saved so that we can spend eternity in heaven. Otherwise we would all be bound for Hell. It's simple. Give it a try. ***...that if you confess with your mouth Jesus as Lord, and believe in your heart that God raised Him from the dead, you will be saved; for with the heart a person believes, resulting in righteousness, and with the mouth he confesses, resulting in salvation (Romans 10: 9, 10).***

Salvation is a free gift, and all we have to do is to believe that Jesus is the son of God who came into the world to die for all sins. It's all a free gift, a freedom that comes with repentance. Now that's love!

Chapter 1
The Decision

"Get away from me and leave me alone! I'm tired," my husband told my autistic, non-verbal, thirteen year old son, Dale.

I was sick and tired of the mental abuse that Dan visited on Dale and me. He was my second husband and he just hated Dale. Dan was easily provoked and had an anger problem; and Dale and I were paying for it.

Dan wanted us to have a baby, and I had always wanted another child, but I could not have a baby with a man who hated my son, especially a mentally handicapped one. Now, I felt like I had two children and it was more than I could bear.

He also, didn't like to work. The only way we could purchase anything was with the good credit I had established. Before meeting Dan, Dale and I had lived in a trailer house and I had struggled to pay for it and pay for my little car. I had good credit because I always made sure my bills were paid. After I married Dan, we lived in my trailer house until we sold it and used the money for down payment on a house in Memphis, Tennessee.

Now, I had a decision to make. It was either going to be my husband or my son. Many other women have had to make similar decisions regard-

Sheila Shelton

ing step fathers. A lot of thoughts went through my mind. Working a part-time job for an airline, I didn't know how I was financially going to make it on my own, but I would not allow Dale to be physically or mentally abused any longer.

 All Dale wanted was a little attention and Dan never paid any positive attention to him. I realized my marriage to Dan was a mistake almost right away. I should have waited a little longer to see how he would act when he was around Dale in different situations, but regretfully I didn't do this. Before the marriage Dan was completely different with Dale. Now I had a hard decision to make.

 A child, especially a mentally handicapped one who just needed a little love and attention shouldn't have to put up with this. They have enough problems. Dan would complain that we couldn't do anything or go anywhere because of Dale. The truth was we couldn't afford to go anywhere, because Dan work enough to help pay all the bills. Now, we were also, facing bankruptcy, ruining my good credit for seven years before I could start again.

 I decided to go ahead and file for divorce, not knowing what the future held for Dale and me. Life was financially hard without Dan, but now Dale and I had peace of mind. I was still worried and anxious, but at least my son was no longer mistreated. We had only been married a short time, but it had been a miserable four years. I felt cheated of not having another child, which I had wanted so desperately. Dan was only in our life a short time, but he managed to do everything, but destroy us. I have never regretted the decision to get him out of our lives.

    I had been lonely in the marriage and now I was even more alone. Paying bills was hard and I had no one to depend on; and I never received any help from anyone. I felt like I had the burden of the world on my shoulders. Ricky was Dale's biological father. He left me before Dale was born and I only received two twelve dollar child support checks, because I was told he was not working and there was no one to investigate this.

    What really hurt is when I learned that Ricky had been married two more times after he left me and the Lord had sent him three more precious children. I was jealous, because the Lord had given him more children after abandoning Dale. I felt so alone, but looking back, I knew the Lord was with Dale and me or we would not have made it. God is so good! God became my provider and I have learned to depend on Him for everything. We didn't have everything, but we had enough.

Chapter 2
My Childhood

I grew up the oldest of five girls and was born in 1954. Lisa, my youngest sister was born in 1964, ten years later. My mother was a stay at home mom and took care of us five girls while my dad worked. I'm so thankful for stay at home moms.

In the early days, after school every day, she would welcome us home with a big smile and always acted so proud to see us. When we were little, until I was nine years old, we didn't have a television and my mom would listen to several preachers on the radio daily. She created a warm, loving, and protective atmosphere in our home.

When I was nine years old, my family moved to Memphis and then to Southaven, Mississippi. That year I attended three different schools which was very hard on me and shook my confidence. My grades in school declined and I started to believe that I was a failure.

Being the oldest of five girls, I was a tomboy and had played with my third cousin, Bruce who was several months younger than me until we moved away when I was nine years old. After moving away from Bruce, I was just lost and it was hard to make female friends and all of a sudden start acting like a girl. I loved the outdoors. I felt like the most

Sheila Shelton

misunderstood person in the world and went into a deep depression. I was just lost. I have suffered with depression most of my life and to make matters worse my parents were very strict; and more is almost always expected from the oldest child.

After moving to Southaven, we had neighbors in the cove in front of our house that had four sons, and I started playing with them, and I felt like my old self again, but at the age of twelve, my dad told me that I was too old to play with boys. I didn't understand this. His decision felt like punishment.

My sister Debbie and I both trusted in Jesus and were saved the same night when she was nine years old and I was ten during a tent revival in Southaven, Mississippi. We believed that Jesus is the Son of God and died on the cross in our place. We both prayed and asked Him to forgive us for all our sins; past, present and future, and come into our lives and save our souls. I have always believed in Jesus, and that He is the Son of God and the only path to Heaven. I thank God that my parents always took us to church.

The Christian denomination I was raised in didn't teach us to praise the Lord every day. They didn't teach us about the power of the Holy Spirit. Needless to say, I lived a defeated life and for years I was suicidal. I also, had a learning disability in school and was so hyper that it was hard to sit still and concentrate, making it difficult to learn. I barely passed. I was never tested nor did they understand ADHD back then, but I'm sure I had it.

The Miracles In My Life

At age twelve, I started babysitting for different families, making fifty-cents an hour. I later raised my price to seventy-five.

I never did get to participate in any school activities and I wanted to so bad. I would probably have enjoyed school a lot more if I had.

Growing up I came to feel like an outcast and little understood or listened to. I felt separated from everyone else. Although I look back at photographs and realize I was pretty I also felt ugly. When I got older I discovered makeup which I tended to over-use. At home, I just needed my privacy, but there were seven of us living in a three bedroom house, which made this impossible. It was hard being the oldest of five girls and my parents expected more out of me than they did the others. This hurt my feelings.

But, the friends I did make in school I made for a lifetime. We do keep in touch with each other, mostly on face book. Our friend Tommie has managed to keep up with us.

Like all little girls, I always imagined that I was going to find the right man, get married and he was going to make things right in my life. I learned this as part of the culture I grew up in both at home and in the community. It took me years to realize that only the Lord can make things right in our lives.

I always thought that I was too dumb to go to college, because of my learning disability, which I kept a secret. I was so ashamed and didn't understand why learning was so hard for me.

Sheila Shelton

Math concepts were so hard to grasp and I failed this subject. I was even spanked for making a bad grade and to this day, I still struggle with math.

Chapter 3
My Teenage and Early Adult Years

At the age of sixteen, I started dating a guy who raped me in the front seat of his car.

I had always intended to keep myself pure and remain a virgin until I got married, to live the way the Lord intended me to live.

I never did tell my parents or anyone else, because I felt violated and convinced that no man would ever want me. I thought that I was ruined, so I kept seeing him and we would make it right and that eventually he would marry me.

At the time, I didn't understand that a crime had been committed and I felt responsible.

Jim was the first guy that my dad allowed me to date and no one warned me that this could happen.

Then one day he called and told me that he was seeing someone else and they were going to get married. I was devastated.

Years later, Jim and his wife divorced and he came back and asked me to marry him.

Let us imagine and be in this moment, will you? I had the strength to say no, but he wouldn't take no for an answer.

Sheila Shelton

My parents were very strict on me and I was afraid to tell them, because dating was the only way I would get to go anywhere except to visit my friends.

My dad made me wait until I was sixteen years old to date; and looking back, I'm glad he did. But he didn't want to let me then.

I felt like an animal out of a cage when I got out on my own; and I didn't know how to act or what to expect and regretfully, I made so many mistakes in my lifetime

I am the one to blame for my poor choices.

Even though I had trusted Jesus at the age of ten, I never felt the Lord in my life or that He loved me, but I still loved and believed in Him.

I was wrong. I just didn't know how to pray, depend on Him, praise Him, nor did I expect Him to answer my prayers, living like a person who had no hope.

I convinced myself that sex outside of marriage must be normal, but I was wrong; and I just wish that young people would save themselves for the person the Lord intended for them, because the Bible tells us that sex outside marriage is a sin.

I just had a low self-esteem and thought that no one would ever want me, but having sex outside marriage doesn't make them love you.

It was hard, but I do forgive Jim, because the Lord commands us to forgive each other or He will not forgive us.

The Miracles In My Life

Forgiveness is powerful, bringing numerous blessings, but if we don't forgive them, then we become their slave.

For if you forgive men when they sin against you, your heavenly Father will also, forgive you, but if you do not forgive men their sins, your Father will not forgive your sins. (Matthew 6:14,15)

Now, I was a senior in high school and at the age of seventeen, I met Ricky.

He was kind and patient with me, everything I needed at the time and it wasn't long before I realize that I was pregnant.

My dad was so upset when my mom and our minister told him, that he said that he would have preferred to hear that I was dead.

Then, when my dad talked to me, he told me the same thing, plus more and it took me years to get over this.

As the old saying goes, I jumped out of the frying pan into the fire, and I cried most of the time, but this was not good for my unborn baby.

I did forgive my dad for the painful things that he said to me; and I realized that he was just hurt and he wanted the best for me.

I just needed to feel loved and I do love both my parents with all my heart.

On May 11, 1972, I graduated high school and on May 13, 1972, Ricky and I were married.

We both lived with my parents and four sisters; and things were really stressful for us, so Ricky left and went back to Arkansas.

Backing up, at the age of sixteen, I started working at the Treasury Department Store and worked until I was eight and a half months pregnant.

After I got pregnant, I had a dream that two doctors were standing at the end of my hospital bed telling me that something was wrong with my baby.

Back then, we didn't know the sex of the baby until it was born like they do now and I wanted a boy so bad since I had four sisters.

Now that I was married, I didn't have any medical insurance, so I had to go to a free clinic at the Baptist Memorial Hospital in Memphis, Tennessee to have my baby.

Abortion was out of the question, because we believe that it is murder, and that the soul enters the body at the time of conception. The Lord has a plan for every human life.

But we also, believe that a person can be forgiven of abortion if they ask the Lord and mean it.

"Before I formed you in the womb, I knew you, before you were born I set you apart; appointed you as a prophet to the nations." (Jeremiah 1:5)

I did enjoy being pregnant and concentrating on my unborn baby and feeling the new life moving around inside me, and I was in love with this precious baby already.

My friend, Tommie gave me a nice baby shower and made me a couple maternity tops and I appreciate her so much.

The Miracles In My Life

My Aunt Brenda who lived in Indiana sent her son's crib and some clothes that her son had out grown and I was so grateful.

I felt so loved and life was good.

During this time, Ricky came back to Memphis, to his mom's and was there when our son, Dale was born, but we never lived together again.

Forceps were used to assist in my baby's delivery and he had scratches all over his face, and his little head was pointed. His little face was purple from lack of oxygen.

If the doctors had performed a c-section on me, it would have prevented this.

When my mom saw Dale for the first time, she said that she knew that I had a hard time with delivery.

The following day, the same two doctors that I had dreamed about months earlier were standing at the foot of my bed, telling me that Dale was having seizures and had stopped breathing. I was speechless.

I had never seen these two doctors before, nor have I seen them since.

I was so young and immature that I didn't even know what a seizure was, and I felt so alone. This just couldn't be happening to me.

All day, I was alone in my hospital room without a phone and didn't have any visitors until late that afternoon when my parents came to visit me. Later, Ricky and his friend came.

Sheila Shelton

I needed to talk to someone so bad, especially my mom, but I didn't have a phone in my hospital room and I didn't know what to do.

I was excited about having a boy and I named him Dale Allen Wilson, because Ricky's middle name was Dale.

Two days later, I went home from the hospital, leaving my precious baby in the neonatal ICU unit for about two weeks, not knowing if he was going to live or die, a heart-breaking experience.

Today, Dale is forty years old and has been having trouble since he was born.

When Dale was a few days old and still in intensive care, Ricky left and went back to Arkansas, never to return.

Thank the Lord, Dale did come home from the hospital after two weeks and now I was happy with my little bundle of joy.

This was short lived, because Dale cried day and night, and I would have to rock him to sleep several times a night until he was four years old.

Sometimes, I'd rock him all night long and I couldn't have made it if it hadn't been for my mom. We were both exhausted.

The doctors couldn't figure out what was wrong with him.

Looking back, I wonder if he was having stomach problems, because of his milk or maybe headaches, because of the seizure activities in his brain. That poor little thing sure did suffer.

The Miracles In My Life

Working at The Treasury Department Store, I worked as a stock girl, making one dollar and seventy-seven cents an hour, and had saved enough money to purchase his milk and whatever else he needed until I found another job when Dale was six weeks old.

I started working at Cleo Wrap in Memphis, making samples for salesmen, and before my insurance went into effect, Dale started having uncontrollable seizures, and again when he was three months old.

He was hospitalized at LeBonheur Children's Hospital, where he stopped breathing again, creating more brain damage.

I would go home at night and back to the hospital during the day, praying and begging the Lord to heal my baby.

One night while he was still in the hospital and I was already home, I prayed silently for Dale and I heard the Lord say, **"He's going to be alright."** Wow!

This was the first time that I remember hearing the Holy Spirit's voice…or recognized it.

Thank You, Lord for Your wonderful grace and mercy.

Then Jesus appeared to James, then to all the apostles, and last of all He appeared to me (Paul) as to one abnormally born. (1st Corinthians 15:7,8)

Chapter 4
The Move

Shortly afterwards, my Grandmother Rhea was killed in an automobile wreck.

My dad was the only living son, and his four sisters wanted him to move into her house so in May 1973, my parents, Dale and I moved eleven miles south of Potts Camp, Mississippi to the country.

When I was eighteen years old, I started working at Wurlitzer Piano Factory in Holly Springs, Mississippi, and I purchased my first car when I was twenty or twenty-one.

I would deal with a crying baby almost all night and work all day, and I was physically and mentally exhausted.

Dale started saying a few words before he was a year old and one of his first words was "coke", which I lived to regret.

He also, said "Mama", "ice", and "I love you".

He was hyperactive, but he was such a precious, loving toddler, and he didn't start walking until he was fourteen months old.

My family was all good to Dale, but I couldn't even get on to him or correct him without someone getting mad at me, and I began to resent this.

Around 1976, I purchased a nice trailer house that I had moved on my dad's land, and Dale and

Sheila Shelton

I moved out or he wouldn't even have known who his mother was.

Don't get me wrong, I appreciated everyone loving him and being good to him. I just needed to feel like his mom.

Now, he had his own bedroom with lots of toys and he enjoyed playing with them.

Shortly afterwards, Dale was diagnosed with Autism at the age of three and my mom and I would take him to the University of Mississippi (Ole Miss.) in Oxford, Mississippi once a week.

Children learn by imitating, as do we all, and the psychological department at Ole Miss taught us how to work with him and he started learning.

Dale is non-verbal and I didn't realize that he could understand me until I was talking to a friend and they asked me how he was doing, and I told them that he was autistic and mentally retarded, but later this diagnosis was changed to autism.

He got so mad at me and I realized then that he understood me, and I was ashamed of myself.

Now, I try to choose my words wisely whenever I am having a conversation with someone and he is present, knowing that he is listening.

Dale gave me a dirty look, gritted his teeth and made a loud sound, as if screaming at me. I had to apologize to him.

Later, I told him that I knew he could understand everything that I said to him, but he just couldn't get it out. He kissed me on the check.

Just because someone doesn't talk, it doesn't mean they don't understand, and they need our love and attention more than a so called normal person.

And we know that in all things God works for the good of those who love Him, who have been called according to His purpose. (Romans 8:28)

Chapter 5
Dale's First School

When Dale was four years old, he started going to McDougal Center School in Tupelo, Mississippi, and at first he stayed all week and came home on the weekends.

My mom and I took him and dropped him off the first time and we both cried when we left.

They taught him so much and they were so good to him.

They also, potty trained him and taught me how to get him to go to sleep at night without having to rock him.

When he was at home, they taught me to put him to bed and put a chair beside his bed. I sat in the chair and every-time he tried to get up, I would gently push him back down on his bed. What a relief. Now, we could both get some sleep. Remember, he was four years old at this time.

Chapter 6
Being A Single Mom

Every Friday was payday and I would pay my bills and a lot of times, wouldn't have enough money left to buy my lunch at work.

Financially, I was drained, but I managed to pay all my bills on Friday and by Monday, I'd sometimes only have a dollar left.

At work, I remember sitting in the lunch room with my friends and co workers, watching them eat and I'd be so hungry.

It was so hard being a single mom, but I made sure that Dale was always taken care of and had all his needs met.

Sometimes, I would borrow a little money to get something to eat from a friend at work and pay them back on Monday

They would ask me why I wasn't eating and I'd tell them that I was on a diet. I was too embarrassed to tell them I didn't have the money to buy something to eat.

It was hard watching them eat when I had an empty stomach.

We just can't imagine what the next person is going through.

I always paid my bills and was never behind or late.

Sheila Shelton

My dad let me borrow money two different times to make a trailer payment, but I paid him back in a timely manner.

I always kept my home and car clean, and about every other week, I would mow the yard, while watching Dale at the same time.

Needless to say, I did have a big yard and a lot of times, it was hard to get my mower started and I would pull on the cord until I was exhausted to get it started. I didn't have the money to get it repaired.

Then, I would mow the yard until the mower ran out of gas and I had to start trying to get it started all over again.

I had propane gas and at first, I had a one hundred pound bottle used to heat the trailer and to cook with, but it didn't last long.

When it ran out of gas, I would have to borrow a truck from someone, unhook the bottle from the house, roll it up on the back of the truck and take it to be exchanged for a full one.

After returning home, I'd roll the bottle off the truck and hook it back up.

It took me awhile to hook it up until I realized that the threads on top of the bottle were made backwards.

Later, I was able to rent a big gas tank from the gas company, but then I'd have to worry about how I was going to get the money to fill it up.

At least the gas company would send a truck to fill up this tank.

The Miracles In My Life

I was always in a financial bind and I remember thinking that I would be willing to dig ditches or work harder to be able to have a better income.

I did get a job working harder, making more money and I am so thankful for that.

The doctors encouraged me to get Dale on Medicaid to help with his doctor bills and to help pay for his medicine; and at first they turned him down and when I reapplied, he was approved. It sure did help me out.

Dale teachers told me that he would never be able to learn to ride a bicycle, so I purchased him one and spend the next four years teaching him to ride.

We lived in the country and there were no sidewalks, so I had to push him in the yard or down my parents' long gravel driveway.

I tried to teach him to use the brakes, but was unable to do so. His tennis shoes were his brakes and he was so cute riding his bicycle.

This just goes to show that we can learn what we want to if we use a little determination or if it is important to us.

Our trailer was nice and it had two back doors, but only one would lock, so we had to use a chain on it and I was so afraid that someone would break in that I slept with a gun.

My bedroom was on one end and Dale's was on the other and each had its own bathroom.

Most nights he would come and get in bed with me during the night or early in the morning.

Sheila Shelton

One morning, I remember him climbing in the bed beside me, and he accidentally hit me in the head with my gun.

I thought I had hidden it from him, but evidently it wasn't.

I never bought him a toy gun to play with, because I knew that he wouldn't know the difference between a real one and a play one.

After that incident, I hid the gun in a different place.

Our trailer was so cold and I had a space heater in the bedroom that I would plug in and help warm the house, but we never slept with it on.

One morning I opened my eyes in time to see Dale walk in the bedroom and plug in the heater, and the cord caught fire.

I jumped out of bed and pulled the plug and put the fire out.

This could have been disastrous. I just thank the Lord for His holy protection.

During this time, I was not close to the Lord, even though I was a believer. I lead a defeated life and God seemed so distant from me. I was a baby Christian, not realizing how the Lord loves and protects us.

I couldn't take Dale to church unless they had a nursery, because he would not sit still and be quiet.

Back then country churches had a nursery, but they didn't know how to handle a mentally challenged child. He was such a handful and he still is.

The Miracles In My Life

Today, he goes to church with his caretakers and housemates and he does sat there and listen and I am so proud of him! I am proud of all his accomplishments!

When Dale was little we visited his favorite fast food restaurant, McDonalds, and went to the restroom before we placed our order.

We passed a table where a couple were eating and before I could stop him, he reached out and took one of their fries and put it in his mouth. I was so embarrassed! Maybe this is where the saying, "Keep your eyes on your fries" comes from. I apologized and they understood. Thank God!

Dale also, loved gum and would go through my purse looking for gum, even though he would chew it and swallow it.

One time, we were in Wal-Mart waiting to check out and I looked and Dale had his hand in the woman's purse in front of us. Again, I tried to explain that he was looking for gum. Talk about embarrassed! I was again! Thankfully, this woman was very understanding, too.

Time after time, he has embarrassed me, but people have been so forgiving. Hope they stay that way, because he still embarrasses me sometimes.

Dale has always been so loveable. He will hug and kiss my hand if he wants me to buy him a Coke, and he treats his caretakers in his group home the same way.

Sheila Shelton

A lot of autistic people are not loveable and cannot stand to be touched, but we just have to accept people the way they are.

When he was little, my family was so good to him and they would give him what he wanted. They still are, especially my sister, Lisa Windham. She has really taken an interest in him over the years.

She would have been good working with mentally challenged children, because she's a natural.

Dale will kiss my check or my hand, especially if he wants something, but being autistic, he doesn't want anyone to kiss him. But he will let me kiss his hand.

It's not easy being a single parent, but as I look back, I can see the Lord was watching over us or we wouldn't have made it. I do wish that I had made wiser choices and had always put the Lord first in everything. Then He would have made things easier for us. I was so blind.

Ricky, Dale's dad and I both made bad decisions, but I feel like we have forgiven each other. He's a good man and still lives in Arkansas. He suffers with severe health problems and has had more than one heart attack. I wish him well.

Chapter 7
My Second Marriage

Dale was around eight years old when I had married Dan.

My sister, Freda introduced me to him when she was dating her future husband, Phil.

Dan stated the fact that he had studied autism in college and knew all about it.

When Dale was younger, I didn't feel like anyone would ever want him or me, a woman with a non-verbal, autistic son, but Dan acted like he loved us so we were married on September 3, 1983, in a church full of family and friends.

At one time, I dated a guy who told me that there was nothing wrong with Dale, he was just spoiled.

Dan and I went to Gatlinburg, Tennessee for our honeymoon and we really enjoyed it.

Our motel room was by a river and at night, we could hear the water.

He was so nice to me and I imagined that life with him would be a good one.

Soon after our marriage, I realized that Dan was jealous of Dale and he wanted us to have a baby. I just couldn't have a child with a man who didn't want my son and acted like one himself.

Sheila Shelton

Dale was afraid of Dan and didn't like to be alone with him, and I resented the way he treated Dale.

He had lied to me, saying that he accepted Dale before I married him. How could I have been so blind to this?

Dale started have uncontrollable seizures again and spent several days in LeBonheur Children's Hospital in Memphis, Tennessee, with an IV in his arm.

One day he jumped up on the bed and pulled the IV out of his arm and I knew he was going to be alright. He always has been tough.

I had known that Dale could only go to school at McDougal Center in Tupelo until he was fourteen years old and then, at that time, Mississippi didn't have anything else for autistic children and I had worried about it.

I had prayed about it and wanted Dale to get the best education that he could.

When he was younger, he stayed at school all week and would come home on weekends. Now, he was coming home every day.

My sister, Lisa was still in high school and she would take him to New Albany, Mississippi to meet the bus every morning, then she would go back and pick him up in the afternoon after school.

After she got out of school, others would use my car to take Dale to meet the bus, and then bring him home him home in the afternoon.

The Miracles In My Life

    I worked in Holly Springs, Mississippi, the opposite direction Dale was going and it was sometimes difficult to find someone to drive him to school.

    Now, Dale was in LeBonheur Hospital again and one of his nurses shared with me that she also, had a son who had autism and about the school in Memphis, called Raineswood that her son went to.

    Raineswood was supported by one of the local churches in the community.

    I have to admit that Dale was a handful and he loves the soft drink, Coke and I used to give it to him to calm him down. Boy, did I have a lot to learn! Seizures and caffeine do not go together and I would never give Coke to a toddler or small child again.

    My family didn't drink tea when I was growing up, so we would drink Coke.

    Now, I purchase Diet-Caffeine free Coke for him, but most machines do not have them and he runs straight to the machines.

    I think it was Friday when Dale was released from the hospital and on Monday, Dan wanted me to go with him to Memphis, Tennessee to look for a job.

    I asked him if we could go by Raineswood School to check it out and we did and we talked to one of the administrators and liked what we saw. It was exactly what Dale needed.

    When we were leaving the school we turned left on Winchester Road and there was a house FOR SALE by owner.

Sheila Shelton

We stopped and asked if we could see it and discussed the price with the owner.

I had been praying for quite some time asking the Lord for a house.

Don't get me wrong, I was so thankful for the trailer that we lived in and had paid for it myself, but my desire was for a house.

Dan and I talked to the owner of the house and told him that we would purchase the house if we could sell the trailer, because we would need the money for a down payment.

We put it up for sale that Monday and on Wednesday, sold it and moved to Memphis that same week.

Talk about God's perfect timing and will, it all happened so fast, because it was God's will and plan for our lives.

When it's God's will, things just fall into place.

Wait for the Lord; be strong and take heart and wait for the Lord. (Psalm 27:14)

Dale enjoyed Raineswood School and later, he went to Avon School.

He always had dedicated teachers who taught him so much. When he learned to drink out of a straw for the first time, was a big deal for us.

Even though he is forty years old now, he still wants five straws or more for his drink. I have to hide them, because it is so funny and people get tickled when they see all his straws. I used to try to stop him, but I just realize it's just who he is.

The Miracles In My Life

Now, I was driving back and forth to Holly Springs, Mississippi to work daily at Wurlitzer Piano Factory, about forty miles one way.

I was only making five dollars and six cents an hour and was paying someone fifty-five dollars a week just to put Dale on the school bus in the mornings.

In the afternoon, I would have to fly home after work and try to beat the school bus.

Some days the bus would be sitting in front of my house, waiting on me so they could drop Dale off and this was so nerve wrecking for me.

School was getting ready to be out for the summer months and I didn't know what I was going to do with Dale, so I quit my job after working at Wurlitzer for eleven years.

I thought that I would be able to draw my unemployment, because I couldn't find a safe, adequate care for my disabled son, but the state of Mississippi didn't see it that way and would they would not help me.

When Dale was twenty-two years old, he and his class graduated with the normal children from Bartlett High School in Bartlett, Tennessee, where he now lives in a group home.

My parents, Terrell and Mary Rhea went to the graduation with my four sisters, Debbie Fair and her daughters, Morgan, Melissa and Mindy; my sister, Sylvia Rhea: my sister Freda Bowling and her oldest son, Justin; and also, my sister, Lisa Windham. I

Sheila Shelton

appreciated all them going so much! It was a joyful occasion.

> ***Delight yourself in the Lord and He will give you the desire of your heart. (Psalm 37:4)***

Chapter 8
MY NEW JOB

After being off work for a year, I put my application in at American Airlines as a Fleet Service Clerk and was hired May 25, 1985.

I always loved airplanes and being around them and it was a desire of my heart that the Lord gave me.

It was an exciting job and I loaded and unloaded airplanes, but it was hard, and the weather was difficult.

Working outside, I didn't know how to dress and the first winter, I almost froze to death.

Later, friends told me that I needed to wear fleece clothing to keep warm and I prepared myself for the cold winters.

At home, I was dealing with a mentally handicapped son, taking care of the house and dealing with an angry husband who didn't want to work.

Nothing seemed to be working out in Dale and my lives.

Why hadn't I waited on the Lord instead of marrying this man who was making our lives so miserable?

And we know that in all things God works for the good of those who love Him, who have been called according to His purpose. (Romans 8:28)

Sheila Shelton

If I had been in my Bible every day, then I might have realized all of this before I made so many mistakes.

One day Dan told me that we were going to file for bankruptcy, because we couldn't pay all our bills.

That is when I decided to file for divorce even though I was only working part time and caring for Dale.

Dan didn't work half the time and was always turning down runs for his truck.

I was so lonely, but I was lonely when Dan and I had been together.

At least now, Dale didn't have to be around him, putting up with his mental and physical abuse, and now we were free.

I had always dreamed of having a good Christian husband and other children, and maybe someday having grandchildren, and I started wondering if something was wrong with me.

I love the Lord and I still went to church, but I had stopped praying and reading my Bible, because I felt hopeless, as if the Lord didn't care anything about Dale and me. Why was everything all so hard?

Now, I was married to Dan and things had gotten worse.

I wished that we had received counseling prior to our marriage, but we didn't.

The Miracles In My Life

Since he didn't work half the time, the only way we could purchase anything was with my good credit, that I had worked so hard to build up.

He had purchased a one ton truck, an eighteen wheeler, and a van for his work, but like I said before, he was refusing to go to work.

He'd lie and tell his place of employment that his truck was out of service or some other excuse.

I would listen to him talk on the phone, whenever he was talking to anyone, wondering what lie he was going to tell next, but I never mentioned it to him until the end.

Dan's first cousin sold real estate and she talked us into purchasing a lot in the Lakeland, Tennessee area, and we could have made a considerable amount of money, but we lost it, because we couldn't pay the payments.

If I asked Dan for lunch money for Dale, he would get upset.

He'd go to work, make a good check, and then stay off until all the money was gone. Then he'd say, "I'm not making any money". I'd explain to him that we were paying bills, but he didn't see it that way.

Sometimes, he would be off on a run and I'd make the mistake of telling him that I just finished mowing the lawn and he'd park his truck somewhere, get on an airplane and fly home for several days.

Sheila Shelton

Since I now worked for an airline, the money for travel was cheaper and would always come out of my paycheck.

He hated mowing the yard or anything else, because he was lazy.

The last time that he flew home like this, he left his truck in New Jersey and flew to Nashville before changing planes and flying on to Memphis. He called to tell me to pick him up at the airport and I told him that he might not want to come home, that I had filed for divorce.

When he got home we fought for four days before he flew back to get his truck. He said that I could have the house, because he didn't want to pay for it.

Dan had wonderful, good Christian parents who adopted him when his dad was fifty years old, and they loved him so much that he was literally spoiled. They are now deceased. His mom died one year and the following year, his dad passed away when he was one hundred years old. I was fortunate enough to be able to attend both their funerals.

Dan remarried and this woman had two sons, and he was jealous of both of them and she also, divorced him.

I would suggest that everyone talk through their problems, respecting the other person's opinion and not let things build up.

The Miracles In My Life

Some people cannot be fixed, except for a miracle of God and a family that prays together stays together.

Always put the Lord first and He will work things out for you. Regretfully, we didn't.

Dan and I went to church together before we were married, but afterwards, he started complaining about it, saying that he needed his rest. Rest from what?

I do forgive him and wish him the best, even though I have no idea where he is or what has happened to him.

I realize that we all have to forgive or the Lord will not forgive us of our sins, and it pleases the Lord when we do forgive others.

For if you forgive men when they sin against you, your heavenly Father will also, forgive you. But if you do not forgive men their sins, your Father will not forgive your sins. (Matthew 6:14,15)

Chapter 9
Dale's Behavior

Dale's behavior kept getting worse and I'd call his Pediatric Neurologists at LeBonheur Hospital and he kept telling me to add another pill for his behavior, but he kept getting worse and not better.

He ran out of the school and around the block twice and his poor teacher had to chase him down and he also, ran in front of two cars while being chased.

While riding the school bus on the interstate, he opened the back emergency door twice; and transportation refused to transport him to and from school.

During the night, Dale would run through the house hollering and upset. I just didn't know what to do and I was mentally and physically exhausted. Neither Dale nor I got any rest and I had to work during the day. I felt like a walking zombie.

I had to have him at the baby sitters at six so I could be at work at six-thirty in the mornings.

By the grace of God, my Avon lady told me about a baby-sitter named Carol, and she was more than willing to take care of Dale and she was a good one.

By now, Dale was sixteen years old and upset all the time and I was stressed out.

Sheila Shelton

We were on our own now, but there was never any peace, because now he was going through puberty.

It was different when he was little, but now he was as tall and strong as me.

Dale stopped talking when he was a little over a year old, after he had his baby shots, and it was hard to communicate with him, much like a stroke patient.

I didn't know what was going on with him, or if he was in extreme pain.

One time, he cried for a few days and I thought he was having an ear ache, but I didn't have the money to take him to the doctor. Then when I did, his ears were fine and his pediatrician told me that it might be his teeth, so I took him to the dentist and the poor little thing had a bad tooth.

This broke my heart and I felt like I didn't have any control at all, and our world just seemed to be crumbling.

I cannot imagine how he has suffered in different ways, but could not tell me.

His teachers didn't want to teach him sign language, because they thought it would discourage him from talking.

This was a mistake and it would have been so much easier if they had. He does know a few simple signs and for this I am thankful.

I believe that sign language should be taught in the school to every student, because you never

The Miracles In My Life

know what situation a person or a loved one is going to wind up in.

Dale was also, having a hard time at school, because of his behavior and his teachers told me that he was going to get killed if I didn't do something about him, and they helped me to get him in Arlington Developmental Center (ADC) in Arlington, Tennessee as an emergency case.

My good friend, Tommie Fernstrom and her daughter, Jennifer, went with me to take Dale to ADC the first time and drop him off.

It was the hardest thing I ever had to do and I was so lonely for my precious son, the light of my life.

It seems to me like mentally challenged children need their parent more than normal ones.

Today at forty years old, he's still a Mama's boy, just like a four year old, but I'm not complaining.

After Tommie, Jennifer and I dropped Dale off at ADC, we had a wreck on the return trip home. A woman was changing lanes on a wet road, and didn't realize that there is a blind spot on the right side of the car, and she pulled in front of me and I slid into her. Thankfully, no one was hurt.

It was devastating leaving Dale and it just broke my heart and I cried a lot, but when I went back to visit him, he was completely different.

Dr. Jones at ADC said that Dale was on so much medication that he didn't know what he was doing so he started taking him off some of it.

Sheila Shelton

On my first visit, Dale was actually smiling and we were so proud to see each other.

I hated for him to have to stay at ADC, but now his medication was being monitored daily and he was receiving the care that he needed, and was also, safe.

Even though I missed him terribly, I always visited him on one of my days off, and we would ride around and spend quality time together.

Chapter 10
Church

During this time, I started going to a non-denominational church and joined the Singles Bible Study, which we had every Tuesday evening.

This church was different from the one I was raised in and I began to learn so much about the Bible and the Lord, and I met some good Christian friends, including my good friend, Melba Kinnin, among others.

Although I had always gone to church, this was different and it really impacted my life.

I began to realize how much the Lord does love Dale and me, and that He has been with us all along.

The Bible tells us that God doesn't judge the outside of a person, but judges our hearts. These people in this church didn't judge the outside appearance and I could see Jesus when I looked at these precious people.

The more I learned about the Lord, the more the Lord started doing thing in my life.

He was trying to mold me into the person He wanted me to be so that I would be more like Him, and now I was beginning to see this.

It was a life changing event, a revelation concept.

Sheila Shelton

He was also, teaching me to worship and praise Him all during the day and night. He wants to be loved, too.

I am a child of God, a princess, because I am a child of the living King Jesus is almost more than my mind can comprehend. It's awesome!

I met Pete Shelton at work and I was in love with him, and over time, things began to work out for us.

We didn't live the kind of life that the Lord wanted us to live and it was so painful from the beginning, but I know that the Lord can take the bad and turn it around to the good.

I know that the Lord can forgive us of our sins if we sincerely ask Him, and we did.

Pete is the man of my dreams and he is such a good Christian, and everything I had ever wanted. I love and respect him so much. He is my best friend.

We went to different churches, but after we started dating, we now go together and we were married on February 14, 2013, Valentines' Day of this year.

I always wanted to get married on Valentines Day because it was my parents' wedding anniversary, and also, my sister, Lisa and Lee's anniversary.

Valentines' Day is also, one of my favorite cousin's, Carolyn's birthday.

I would advise every teenager to pray that the Lord would send you a good Christian spouse and then wait on the Lord to do so. It will save you from a lot of heartaches, because He does have the right person picked out for you.

The Miracles In My Life

The Lord does tell us to wait until marriage to have sex and I wish that I had. It also, makes it so special and you will be blessed for it.

I have been so foolish and have made so many mistakes in my life, because I didn't wait on the Lord.

Chapter 11
New Friends Enter our Lives

I was visiting Dale every week while he was at Arlington Developmental Center (ADC), and would ride him around and if I had the money, we'd go shopping, looking or just walking in the mall.

I remember that I would be so lonesome and I wondered if this was the way it was always going to be, and I prayed and told the Lord how lonely I was.

Dale is non-verbal, but I talk to him about everything I can think of, even telling him what road, street, highway or interstate we are on.

One day when I was visiting him at ADC, I met Judy Parker and her son, Charlie who also, lived at ADC, and the Lord just put us together.

It was divine intervention, and it has been wonderful.

I now have someone to talk to and we understand each other, and each other's sons, and now we are family.

We ride around, shop together, take our boys out to eat, and we have taken them on vacations, and Judy and I are so much alike. We can tease each other and not get mad and she is just a delight to be around…and so is Charlie. We are all so comfortable together.

Judy is writing a book on our families and the things that our precious sons have done, some good and some not so good.

One example of this would be when we took them on vacation to Gatlinburg, Tennessee and we had to make a potty stop.

Like I said earlier, Dale is a Coke-a-holic and he knows the difference between Coke and Pepsi, which he will not drink.

I had to purchase him a Coke, because he would not leave the drink machine, and now he held out for two, one for each hand. He doesn't need them, because of his seizures and an acid stomach.

I was trying to get him to leave and people were looking at me like, "What are you doing to that poor young man?" I was so mad at him!

It's funny now, but it sure wasn't then.

We were also, embarrassed when we were in Wal-Mart, and some man said "Do you know this man?" He was talking about Charlie. He said, "He hugged my wife".

Well, Charlie hugs everyone and he is loveable, but we have to watch him around women, especially if they have a cleavage. That's pretty normal, isn't it! He hugs men, too.

We had to do some fast explaining to this man. Charlie just likes friendly people, and they know who likes them and who doesn't.

The Miracles In My Life

Needless to say, we still have to watch Charlie around the women.

Thank you, Lord for Your sense of humor when You gave us Dale and Charlie. It hasn't been easy, but I know that You have helped us in every situation. Lord, I bet You also, get a chuckle out of watching them sometimes. You are truly an awesome God!

Chapter 12
Unique Personalities: Gifts From God

Dale and Charlie both have unique personalities and have embarrassed us so many times.

Several times over the years, we have taken them out to eat and if the waitress didn't refill Dale's drink quick enough, he would get up, go behind the counter and refill his own.

I got so mad at him and he just looked at me like, "What's the problem?"

How are you going to control a grown man? It's impossible.

When we are riding around, I drive and Dale sits behind, and Charlie sits behind Judy on the right side.

Charlie is unable to put his seatbelt on so we tell Dale to buckle him up, and when we stop, we tell Dale to let Charlie out and he does.

Those boys complement each other in their everyday lives and they are so special.

A lot of times, Dale will poke me when we pass a store or a fast food restaurant, wanting me to stop and purchase him a drink, even if he has one in his hands.

Sheila Shelton

He loves straws and will use five or six for one drink. I just don't know what the deal is, but he does, and when are shopping, and he sees straws, he will grab them and place them in the basket for me to purchase.

Charlie keeps his eyes on the road and seems to know where we are and when we head back towards their home in Bartlett, no matter where we are, he starts shaking his head no, because he wants to keep riding. He would have made a good truck driver. His sense of direction just amazes us.

Judy and I look back and laugh at all the incidences that we have been fortunate enough to live through.

One time Judy and I took Dale and Charlie to Taco Bell, which we love, but they have Pepsi products.

We received our order and sat down to eat; and Dale tasted his drink. It was Pepsi.

He got up and went to the counter and tried to tell them that he wanted Coke. He is non-verbal, but he sure did try. I got mad at him and felt sorry for him at the same time. He can take the Coke and Pepsi challenge and win, because he knows the difference in the taste.

When we ride around, he will let me know that he has to go to the restroom and when I stop to take him in, he runs straight to the drink machines or to the counter in the fast food restaurants.

The Miracles In My Life

I started taking a urinal with us every time we ride around, because I get tired of him outsmarting me.

Every week when we take them out, I take two small bottled, diet-caffeine-free Cokes. Dale will drink his and want Charlie's. We have to watch him, because he is sneaky.

We took them on vacation to Chattanooga, Tennessee a couple of times and went to the aquarium.

Judy is seventy-four years old and she's on a walker, because a drunk driver ran into her and her husband several years ago, and messed her back up. She's still in a lot of pain.

When we went to the aquarium, we put her in a wheelchair and Charlie wanted to push his mom around so we let him.

Dale, Charlie and I walked up the hill and when we arrived at the top, Charlie let her go, sending Judy barreling down the hill. Well, guess who had to chase her down? I did. It was funny after I caught her. I can fun fast when I have to.

We also, went to the IMAX Theater in Chattanooga and after we were seated, Dale let me know that he needed to go to the restroom.

When we got to the women's restroom, it was blocked off and they were cleaning the men's. I had to go, too.

There was a cleaning man standing at the entrance and I told him that Dale needed to go to the restroom and he told us to go ahead, and I could go in to help him if I needed to, that he would stand at the door to keep anyone from going in.

Dale still has to have help with toilet tissue, so I went in to help him and also, used it myself.

Before we finished, I heard men's voices and when we came out of the stall, the culprit guarding the door had disappeared.

When we were passing the urinal, there were two men with their backs to us, using the restroom. Their eyes were big as raccoons when they saw me.

I thought that I needed to explain why I was in the men's restroom, and then I thought, "We have got to get out of here." But I did manage to speak. I was so ashamed!

Needless to say, that was one time Dale and I did not wash our hands until we arrived at our car and used the sanitizer.

Years earlier when Dale was about seven years old, I had a little Ford Fiesta car which was good on gas.

We were visiting my parents one day and were leaving when I thought of something that I forgot to tell my dad, so I told Dale to go ahead and get in the car.

As I turned around and walked away, I heard the car crank up and as I looked back, the car headed towards the road with Dale sitting in the back seat.

I started screaming at the top of my lungs for the little car to stop, and I had to chase it down. It's a good thing that I can run fast as I was praying,

The Miracles In My Life

and I finally caught up with the car and managed to jump in and stop it

The car was a four speed and when I would start it without putting my left foot on the clutch, would usually go dead, but this time it didn't.

Dale knew that the key had to be on for him to listen to the radio, which he was trying to do.

When he was younger and riding the school bus home from school, he took his tennis shoes off and threw them out the window. The driver stopped the bus, but was unable to find them.

One day Lisa, my sister, Dale and I had been shopping in New Albany, Mississippi and were going home.

The air-conditioner wasn't working and we had the windows down. Dale was sitting in the back seat and got hot so he took his shirt off and threw it out the window.

Of course, I had to stop and pick it up. He keeps me on my toes.

Charlie's dad, Sam, used to let him ride the lawn mower with the blade up, and when he would get off, it would go dead. (His dad has been dead for several years now.)

One day Charlie was driving it and put the blade down. He mowed down the Azalea bushes and several other plants before they could stop him.

Judy said that he was so proud of himself and she thought it was funny, but Sam was not impressed.

Sheila Shelton

One day, Dale, Charlie, Judy and I went by her house and she wanted to let me see him driving the lawn mower in the yard, so she got it started for him.

After he drove it around for a while, he got off, but the mower kept going. Well, guess who had to chase it down? I did. Sometimes I wonder if the Lord gets a chuckle out of watching us. It is comical now.

These are just a few things that have happened to us and it's a good thing that Judy and I have a good sense of humor.

If you happen to see two elder ladies, one on a walker and they have two mentally handicapped sons with them, well, it's a possibility it just might be us. If you watch long enough, you might get a good laugh. It's a circus sometimes.

It can be nerve wrecking with Dale walking around looking for a Coke, and Charlie trying to hug all the women.

We do a lot of praying while we go through our activities, and the Lord always helps us.

I am so thankful that we never gave up on our sons. The Lord doesn't make mistakes, even though we do. And these boys are such a blessing to us.

Every human being is created in the image of God and for a divine purpose and no one is a mistake in God's eyes. God knew you before you were born. You are here for a purpose.

Chapter 13
Miracles

The Lord has shown me so much in my lifetime and I just want the readers to be able to recognize their blessings, because they are always there.

Regretfully, I have made so many mistakes in my lifetime, but I have learned to depend upon the Lord in every situation and know that He is faithful.

Commit to the Lord whatever you do, and your plans will succeed. (Proverbs 16:3)

Every Christian has the Holy Spirit inside of us, who seals us for the Day of Redemption, and helps us in our everyday lives.

We have to pray and give our burdens to the Lord, because we are not equipped to handle them. They would literally drive us crazy.

Just watch and see what the Lord will do when you put your burdens in His hands. He sure has taken good care of Dale, Charlie, Judy and me.

Airplane Crashes

For years, even before I started working at the airport, I dreamed of airplane crashes.

I don't know why, but a lot of times, I even dreamed that an airplane crashed in front of the airport in Memphis.

Sheila Shelton

I haven't dreamed this since I started praying for the safety of the airplanes; and I do believe in the power of prayer.

Lord, thank You so much for keeping the airplanes safe.

And I (Jesus) will do whatever you ask in My name, so that the Son may bring glory to the Father. (John 14:13)

Alaska

I worked for American Airlines until I retired on December 1, 2012, and was blessed to be able to visit Alaska five times.

Two of these times, I was fortunate to be able to take my parents, Terrell and Mary Rhea with me.

My uncle had retired from the Air Force and he and my aunt would spend their summers there where he would sell real estate, and the weather was cooler than it was in their home in Virginia.

Before my parents and I left, I had such a dreadful feeling. I prayed that the Lord would give us a safe trip and let us have a good time.

We had a wonderful, uneventful time and as we boarded the airplane about one o'clock in the morning for our return trip home, that same dreadful feeling came over me again.

I started praying and the Lord said, **"Start praising Me"**, so I did.

I sat in an aisle seat on the left side, close to the back of airplane, next to a woman and her hus-

The Miracles In My Life

band. They kept talking and I just wanted to go to sleep. They were such a nice couple.

All of a sudden an airplane zoomed right past us on the left side, heading in the opposite direction that we were traveling.

I told the woman seated next to me that I had had a bad feeling about that flight and had prayed for our safety, and she said that she had felt the same way and had also, prayed.

I looked out the window and there was a line of angels all the way down by the side of the airplane! I just couldn't believe it! It was totally amazing! Awesome!

The angels were all white as a sheet, and I could see the forms of their bodies, arms and legs, and they were holding hands, protecting us.

I could not see their eyes or facial features, only their body forms and I believe that God had intentionally kept me awake so that my new friends and I could see the great miracle that He had performed for us.

Thank You for Your awesome protection, Lord!

"Because he loves me", says the Lord, "I will rescue him; I will protect him for he acknowledges My name..." (Psalm 91:14)

A Hedge Of Protection

Years ago, one of the pastors and his wife in our church where I attended, moved out of state and after a couple of years returned to the Memphis, Tennessee area.

They lived in an apartment until they found their house.

Every night before they went to bed, they would pray that the Lord would put a hedge of protection around their apartment.

One night all the surrounding apartments burned, but thank God, theirs was spared.

The apartments beside and over them burned, but they only received a little smoke damage.

Thank You, again, Lord for Your awesome protection. You are truly an amazing God.

Hath thou not made a hedge about him, and about his house, and above him, above his house, and above all that he has on every side? Thou hath blessed the work of his hands, and his substance is increased in the land. (Job 1:10)

Almost Had A Wreck

Several years ago, my mom was in the hospital, recovering from Colon Cancer Surgery,

This was when my son, Dale was in Arlington Developmental Center (ADC), because his behavior had gotten so bad.

I wanted Dale and my mom to be able to see each other.

The weather was supposed to get bad that day, so I decided to pick Dale up, take him to the hospital for a visit, then return him to ADC, which

The Miracles In My Life

was in Arlington, Tennessee, about thirty miles from where I lived.

Dale is non-verbal, but he understands when I say, "Let's pray" he always gives me his hand and I pray for our safety, before we leave in the car.

We had a nice visit at the hospital with my parents, and were on our way back to ADC on interstate forty, when we hit black ice and were all over the interstate.

I tried tapping the brakes, but nothing I did corrected the problem.

I thought about the prayer that Dale and I prayed before we left the hospital, so I prayed again and the Lord said, **"Lock it up."**

In my mind, I knew that this was not logical, but I obeyed the voice of the Lord and locked it up.

When we started out, we were heading east, but when we came to a stop, the nose of the car was pointing to the West towards oncoming traffic.

Thank You, Lord that there were no cars around us.

Dale started laughing.

I just started praising the Lord and thanking Him for His awesome protection.

Growing up, I was not taught the importance of praising the Lord.

I had suffered with depression most of my life, but every time I passed this one spot, I would remember what the Lord did for Dale and me, and I would start thanking and praising Him.

Sheila Shelton

I began to realize how much better I felt when I would praise and thank Him, because we were created to praise the Lord, and I stopped being so depressed, because I realize that praise breaks the bondage, the curses.

This was a great lesson that the Lord taught me and God is so good! It changed my life.

Thank You for Your holy protection again, Father God, and for teaching me to praise and worship You, in Jesus name.

I will praise You, O Lord, with all my heart; I will tell of Your wonders. (Psalm 9:1)

<u>Angel Eyes</u>

My son, Dale and I go to my parents to spend the night occasionally.

Because Dale has seizures and is non-verbal, I sleep in the same room with him even though he is forty years old.

Dale sleeps in the bed and I pull a mattress out from under the bed, make it up, and turn it towards the door and sleep in it.

He woke up during the night and made a sound.

As I was opening my eyes, I looked up above the door and saw eyes looking down at me for a few seconds, and then they disappeared from my sight.

I have always heard that angels are very tall; and I knew that the Lord had allowed me to see

The Miracles In My Life

the angel who was there protecting Dale and me. I was not afraid. I just rejoiced and praised the Lord, and I still get excited every time I think about those eyes.

Who knows, maybe it was one of our guardian angels.

I feel like those eyes are still looking down on me now. I can feel them.

My God is so good and so caring to take such good care of Dale and me like He does!

For He will command His angels concerning you to guard you in all your ways. (Psalm 91:11)

Being Held Down

I had forgotten about this until I heard our pastor saying that this had happened to him.

I would be lying in bed asleep and I would wake up, feeling like something was holding me down, and I would keep trying to talk, but wouldn't be able to and I would have a hard time breathing. This happened so many times.

Finally, I would manage to say, "Jesus" and it would release me.

This hasn't happened in a long time now.

Father God, thank You for there is power in Jesus' name and Christians have the power to use it, because we have the Holy Spirit living inside of us.

Sheila Shelton

Father God, I also, thank You that all we have to do is say, "Jesus, help me" and You send the holy angels to help us in our time of need.

...and call upon Me (Jesus) in the day of trouble; I will deliver you, and you will honor Me. (Psalm 50:15)

<u>Benny Hinn</u>

On day I was home from work and was watching Benny Hinn on Christian television.

After the sermon was over, he said that there was a woman watching who has heart trouble, and the Lord wants to heal you.

I was sitting in my recliner looking down at a magazine while he was talking, when he said that, I looked up.

He said, "She's sitting in a chair, looking at a book, and she just looked up and she probably doesn't even know that she has heart trouble."

He explained what I was doing and how I was sitting, that it made me feel like he was talking about me.

Father God, thank You for taking such good care of us all the time, even when we don't realize it.

I will answer them before they even call on Me. While they are still talking about their needs, I will go ahead and answer their prayers! (Isaiah 65:24)

The Miracles In My Life

Better Than Alright

My nephew, Justin went to prison for selling marijuana. He was sentenced to three years; and it just broke our hearts.

My family and I always prayed for him and while he was there, he read the Bible every day and had a close relationship with our Lord.

One time, I was asking the Lord if Justin was going to be alright and He said, **"He's going to be better than alright."**

Justin worked hard while he was there and got his GED while he was incarcerated; and was back home in seventeen months.

While he was incarcerated, he read his Bible and learned to depend on the Lord completely, and stayed out of trouble. He learned so much about the Lord.

He is still having a few problems today, but I keep remembering God's promises to me, **"He's going to be better than alright"**.

I also, realize that the devil tried to destroy him. The Lord must have big plans for his life.

Thank You, Father God for helping Justin and keeping Your promise, in Jesus name. You are a great God!

I pray the eyes of your heart may be enlightened in order that you know the hope to which Jesus has called you, the riches of His glorious Inheritance to the saints. (Ephesians 1:18)

Sheila Shelton

Bill Died

About four years ago, several people died who my family and I knew, and I remember wondering "Who in the family is going to be next" and my Uncle Bill came to mind.

On April 23, 2008, that same year, his daughter called to tell me that her dad had been killed in an automobile accident.

He was changing a flat tire on the interstate and an eighteen wheeler truck was passing them, avoided a drunk driver coming across the median, had swerved to the right, hitting and killing him instantly.

He was a good Christian man and I will always have fond memories of him. He just seemed to love everyone and was a joy to be around. He made everyone he talked to feel important and he didn't judge or talk about anyone.

Bill would visit nursing homes on Sundays and he would

talk to the patients and he also, witnessed to them.

He was a family man who loved his wife, his mom, his siblings, his children, their spouses and his grandchildren. He would call and visit them on a regular basis, and I respected him for this. All his family looked up to him.

Thank You, Father for the wonderful people you put in our lives.

The Miracles In My Life

But God has revealed it to us by the Spirit. The Spirit searches all things, even the deep things of God. (1st Corinthians 2:10)

Bob

I worked for American Airlines for twenty-five years, and one night I dreamed about Bob, an automotive mechanic we worked with.

I dreamed that he was sick and was off work for twenty-one days and had no idea that he was even having problems.

Sure enough Bob did get sick and was off work the same number of days that I had dreamed of.

Thank you, Lord for healing Bob and please bless him and his family. Help me to pray for everyone You put on my mind.

Is any of you sick? He should call the elders of the church to pray over him and anoint him with oil in the name of the Lord. (James 5:14)

Byhalia, Mississippi

I grew up I Southaven, Mississippi, and my grandparents lived about an hour and a half away.

Before the interstate was built, we would drive though a little town of Byhalia, Mississippi on our way to visit our grandparents and relatives.

Almost every time we'd go through Byhalia, I'd get the strange feeling that there was someone in this town for me, as if something was drawing me to that town. I cannot explain it. This would happen even when I was a young girl.

Now at the age of fifty-eight, I am married to Pete, a wonderful, Christian man from Byhalia who also, goes to church with me.

Wonder if the Holy Spirit was trying to tell me something?

Give thanks in all circumstances, for this is God's will for you in Christ Jesus. (1st Thessalonians 5:18)

Car Ran Off The Road

Before I leave home, I always say my prayers, and ask the Lord to protect me.

One time, I was driving down the road and there was a split with oncoming traffic, so I merged into the left lane.

One of the cars merging onto the road I was traveling, came all the way over in my lane, forcing me off the road.

There was a presence in my car with me, who took over the steering wheel, and helped me to run off the left side of the road to avoid a serious accident.

Lord, again, thank You for your awesome protection! Your holy angels are with me all the time and I know that when I pray, You release them to protect me.

"Have I not commanded you? Be strong and courageous. Do not be terrified, do not be discour-

aged for the Lord your God will be with you wherever you go." (Joshua 1:9)

Carbon Monoxide Poisoning

A few years ago, strong winds came through the Memphis area and thousands of residents were left without power for ten days, including me.

Pete brought his portable gas generator up and hooked it up in my garage, by the back garage door. We did leave the door open.

I was able to watch television, get on my computer and use minimum lights when I was home.

I kept my windows opened, which I usually hate to do, but it was in the summer and the weather was hot, so I lowered the windows and turned the air conditioner on at night.

At night, I would get up and add gasoline to the generator as I did during the day after work.

One day my head started throbbing so I turned my computer on and looked up Carbon Monoxide poisoning on Google, and I had all the symptoms, which were shortness of breath, nausea, dizziness, light headedness and a throbbing head. I thought I was going to die and I was afraid.

When you breathe in Carbon Monoxide, it replaces oxygen in your blood and your heart, brain and body become starved of oxygen, even though you cannot smell it, resulting in death.

I panicked, ran in the garage and turned off the generator, and ran back in the house to use my cordless phone to call paramedics and of course, it didn't work without electricity.

I wasn't thinking clearly and I went to the bedroom and called 9-1-1 on my other phone, and called Pete at work and told him what was going on.

Then, I opened the garage door so the paramedics could get in before I passed out. I was already feeling light headed.

They transported me to the hospital, administering oxygen on the way, which was still very low when we reached the Emergency Room.

If I had waited a little longer, I don't think I'd be here today, but the Lord had a plan for my life.

And we know that in all things, God works for the good of those who love Him, who have been called according to His purpose. (Romans 8:28)

Casting Out Unclean Spirits

One night, I heard a preacher on television talking about casting out unclean spirits from people.

He said you have to be bold and speak with authority, demanding unclean spirits to come out of people…in Jesus' name.

You have to raise your voice to them or they will not leave and the preacher said that you have to tell them to go back to the pit (hell)….in Jesus' name, and you also, have to plead the Blood of Jesus on the person whom you want the demon to leave.

The Miracles In My Life

They have to obey Christians, because we have the power of the Lord, living inside of us.

Demons do not want to go to hell.

The preacher also, said that when we sin, it gives demons power to enter unsaved people, and to come into a Christian's life, controlling them.

He also, said that demons are small, but the more a person sins, the more powerful they become and the bigger they get. They grow with our sins.

They can get so big that they look like gorillas walking around.

Sometimes, when I was working there would be a couple men who were having a loud verbal disagreement, and they would be screaming and yelling at the top of their lungs, as if they were going to have a fist fight.

I would go to the women's restroom where I could be alone and pray, and praise the Lord. Then I would command the demons that were in and around these men to go back to the pit, in Jesus' name. Then, I would say, "Go!". (Praise is just as important as prayer.)

A few minutes later, I would go back to the break room and those men would be talking and laughing, and they would be friends again. It happened this way on numerous occasions, with different people.

Then, I would thank the Lord for what He did.

We need to always thank and praise Him for everything He does for us, for this is the will of the Lord and it pleases Him.

Sheila Shelton

While I was writing this, I couldn't remember the preacher's name who I was talking about and I prayed and asked the Lord his name.

I started to get up and see if I could find it and the Lord said, **"Sit down and I will tell you his name,"** so I sat back down on the bed and the Lord said, **"Kenneth Copeland".**

Lord, thank You for Your power that You gave us to cast out these unclean spirits in Your name. I also, want to thank You for talking to us and all we have to do is listen.

...and His incomparable great power for us who believe. That power is like the working of His mighty strength. (Ephesians 1:19)

<u>Cindy</u>

I hadn't seen my friend, Cindy in quite some time, but we had been friends for years and we used to work together.

One afternoon, I was getting dressed to go to my Singles Bible Study at church, when her sister called and told me that Cindy had passed away. She had committed suicide.

I started to stay home, but I knew the Lord wanted me to attend the Bible study. It was always such a blessing to me.

At church Carol, the preacher's wife laid hands on me and prayed for me.

The Miracles In My Life

The next evening, I went to visitation at the funeral home. As I looked at Cindy in the casket, the Holy Spirit said, **"It's only a shell. She's not there"**.

After the funeral, I was told that she had shot herself at her mom's house and died in the ER at the hospital, and that she had seen demons before she died.

Cindy was divorced and she left a little boy who was about seven years old.

Recently, I became friends with her son on face book and he has two small children, a boy and a girl.

I cried when I saw the pictures of Cindy's grandchildren. She has missed so much.

Father God, thank You for all Your blessings and please help us to be strong and to depend on You for everything.

I consider that our present sufferings are not worth comparing with the glory that will be revealed in us. (Romans 8:18)

Clara Died

One Thursday night, I went to bed, but did not go to sleep until the wee hours on Friday morning of January 28, 2011. I have trouble going to sleep at night.

I dreamed that my dad's ninety three years old first cousin, Clara died.

The next morning, my sister sent me a text message that said, "Clara Garrison died last night".

Sheila Shelton

It was so strange to dream something again and have it to happen

Thank You, Lord that Clara was such a good Christian woman and her life was a living sacrifice for You.

Precious in the sight of the Lord is the death of His saints. (Psalm 116:15)

Cookware

One day I was surfing the channels on the television looking for something to watch, and I stopped on the QVC channel. They were selling beautiful glass cookware which you could also, serve in.

Also, each one came with a rack to put it on and a plastic lid.

I thought, "I sure would like to have that," but I knew that I could not afford it, but I never told anyone.

Well, for Christmas, my friend Melba gave me a two piece set, complete with the serving racks and lip. I was so proud of them!

Thank You, Lord for giving me the desires of my heart. Please bless my good friend, Melba.

But seek first His kingdom and His righteousness, and all these things will be given to you as well. (Matthew 6:33)

Diana

Peggy, one of the precious ladies in our church had a daughter who had been ill for a couple of

The Miracles In My Life

years; and we had been praying for her healing and also, for her salvation.

The daughter lived in another city and the lady in our church had been called out of town, because her daughter had become seriously ill.

I prayed often and had such a burden for Diana.

One night, I was praying and the Holy Spirit gave me the greatest peace. It was if the Lord was telling me that everything was alright now.

The great burden that I felt was completely taken away from me and now, I felt peace about the situation.

After two days, on the morning of December 8, 2011, Diana passed away.

Our minister sent everyone an email telling us about her passing and also, said that Diana's mom had peace about it.

Later, I talked to Peggy and told her that something had happened a couple of nights before her daughter passed away. Her mom said that it was the last night that she had spent with Diana at the hospital and a friend of her daughter, who was now living for God, came in the hospital room and had ministered to her.

Diana and her friend talked about what all God had done for them while the mother sat listening to their wonderful conversation.

With all my heart, I believe that Diana accepted Jesus as her Lord and Savior that night.

Sheila Shelton

"These things have I spoken to you so that in Me (Jesus), you now have peace. In the world you have tribulation, but take courage, I have overcome the world." (John 16:33)

Flying Lessons

I took flying lessons and was able to get my Single Engine Land license to fly in 1995, and I am qualified to fly a Cessna 152 and a 172, even though I haven't flown in quite some time now.

I always loved airplanes and my dream came true. It was the most awesome feeling to be able to do something so spectacular, and I fell so blessed for having been able to do it.

As a child I grew up in Southaven, Mississippi and there used to be an airport across the field. We could watch the small airplanes taking off and landing. My family and I enjoyed watching them and one day, my dad took us to the airport and hired someone to take us all for a ride. It was awesome and I was hooked.

I used to say that I wanted to ride in an airplane before I died and now, the Lord gave me the desire of my heart and I was actually flying one.

Before I got my pilot's license, I was flying downwind preparing to land the little Cessna airplane, and the wind was really strong. It tossed the airplane and I was afraid, so I prayed and asked the Lord to help me and He said, **"Why are you afraid? I am right here with you."**

Then the fear, which is of the devil, left me; and I actually enjoyed being tossed around in the little airplane.

Thank You, Lord for helping me to land safe and for helping me to get my license.

He will cover you with his feathers, and under His wings you will find refuge; His faithfulness will be your shield and rampart (defense). (Psalm 91:4)

Getting Ready For Work

At one time, I had to be at work at four-thirty in the morning and I had to get up at three to get ready.

I washed my face and tried to put my contacts in, but for some reason, I could not get them in. I was so frustrated.

I prayed and asked the Lord to help me, but I still couldn't get them in.

I said, "Ok, Lord, what's going on?" I knew this was going to make me late for work and the Lord always helps me. There must be a reason.

Then, I heard a loud crash outside and I looked out the window, but I didn't see anything.

I tried again and the contact went right in so I finished getting ready for work and left home.

When I got a few feet from my house, I could see that someone had a bad wreck, and the fire department and ambulance were there.

If I had left on time, then I might have been in that wreck, too. I felt like the Lord had protected me, and I am so thankful. I am so blessed!

Sheila Shelton

Thank You, precious Lord for Your awesome protection yet again. You are an amazing God and I love You with all my heart.

The angel of the Lord encamps around those who fear Him and He delivers them. (Psalm 34:7)

<u>Going To Church Along</u>

Pete and I always go to church together and neither one of us had missed a service in over two years.

Eagles Nest Christian Fellowship Church, a non-denominational church means the world to us.

I had started going to church on Saturday nights when I had to work Sunday mornings; and Pete and I kept it up after we retired.

Pete hurt his back and wasn't able to go to church for a while; and I had to go alone.

One afternoon, I was on my way to church and I told the Lord that I was lonely going to church without Pete.

The Lord said, **"I'll be there"**, and sure enough He was…and still is.

I was blessed for going. After Pete had his back surgery, he was able to start going back with me again and thank God, his back hasn't hurt since.

… "and teaching them to obey everything I have commanded you. And surely I am with you always, to the very end of the age." (Matthew 28:20)

Good Morning, Holy Spirit

I read the book that Benny Hinn wrote called <u>GOOD MORNING, HOLY SPIRIT</u> and really enjoyed it, and I used to watch him on his television ministry.

When he would rise in the morning, he would say, "Good morning, Holy Spirit" and the Lord would answer him back, **"Good morning, Benny"**.

So, I tried it, "Good morning, Holy Spirit" and the Lord responded, **"Good morning, Sheila"**.

What an awesome feeling it is to be able to communicate with the God of the universe. We talk to him and now, we just need to listen to his voice, in our hearts and in our minds.

Now I say, "I love You, Jesus" and He always responds, **"I love you, too, Sheila"**. I do this several times a day and also, at night. He loves to hear it, too.

We Christians have the Holy Spirit living inside of us and He is our helper, as well as our seal.

Thank You, Lord, for Your precious Holy Spirit.

As has just been said, "Today, if hear His voice, do not harden your heart as you did in the rebellion." (Hebrews 3:15)

My Great-Grandma

Several years ago, I dreamed that my mom died, but it wasn't my mom; and I did not understand it.

It made me sad, and a few days later, my great-Grandma Robbins died, my mom's grandmother.

Sheila Shelton

Grandma loved the Lord and was a very righteous woman who knew her Bible.

She had the peace of the Lord on her and she always had a smile when we would see her.

Thank You, Lord for the good Christian influence that Grandma had on all who knew and loved her.

I was young when she died, but I will never forget her; and someday, I know I will see her again.

Those who walk uprightly enter into peace; they find rest as they lie in death. (Isaiah 57:2)

He Almost Drowned

One day, Roy, his wife, daughter, son-in-law and two grandsons were having a cookout.

Roy was cooking on the grill and his oldest grandson asked him why the youngest one was lying face down in the bottom of the swimming pool.

He looked and saw the little boy lying face down in the pool, so he jumped in and grabbed the little boy. When he did, he said that he could feel feathers.

He could not explain it and was not a religious man until later, but he did realize that it was an angel.

Roy pulled the little boy out of the pool, revived him, and while he was unconscious, the boy told them what they were all doing while he was in the pool. He had an "out of the body" experience.

Thank the Lord, the little boy was fine, but it made a lasting impact on Roy's life and he never forgot it.

Lord, I know that You do what it takes to get our attention, because You love us so much.

"I am the Lord, the God of all mankind. Is anything too hard for Me?" (Jeremiah 32:27)

Healed

I had been in a lot of pain with the heel of my right foot for some time and had gone to my PCP and had it x-rayed.

Dr. Baker told me that I had a bone spur on my heel, gave me some cream to put on it; and some exercises to do.

Neither helped and I was still in pain.

Pete and I went to church one Saturday night and I thought about not going, so I prayed about it. The Lord said, "**You will miss a blessing if you don't go**", so I decided to go.

It was May 8, 2010, and we had a precious black lady who preached that night. Everyone just loves her.

She was preaching and she stopped and prayed, and said if anyone needed a healing to raise their hands, and I raised mine, as did several others.

Pastor Tina said for all of us who had our hands raised to come up front, so we did.

Sheila Shelton

She came by each person and prayed for us and when she touched my forehead, she asked the Lord to heal me from the top of my head to the bottom of my feet. I thought about my heel. Then, the pain completely went away!

The pain has tried to return several times, but I kept thanking the Lord for healing my heel, and it departed. The devil tries to give the symptoms back to you so you will lose your faith. We cannot listen to him. I refuse to.

My friend, Elizabeth Hill was also, healed that night of COPD. She said that she hadn't been able to take a deep breath in seven years.

Thank You, Father for encouraging me to go to church that night. If I had stayed home, I would have indeed missed a blessing. Because of my obedience, You chose to heal me.

He (Jesus) Himself bore our sins in His body on the tree, so that we might die to sins and live for righteousness; by His wounds you have been healed. (1st Peter 2:24)

Helping Others

Different times, I would be shopping I'd see something that I thought one of my friends might want or need.

I would pray about it and the Holy Spirit would say, **"Sheila, if you thought you were going to die tomorrow, would you buy it?"** I'd say, "Yes, Lord"

The Miracles In My Life

That would be my answer that the Lord wanted me to go ahead and make the purchase. I am not able to do this very often, because I cannot afford it, but I wish I could.

I am not bragging on myself, but on the Lord.

Thank You, Lord for allowing me to give my friends the desires of their hearts, when I am able to do so.

Do not withhold good from those who deserve it, when it is in your power to act. (Proverbs 3:27)

I Do Remember

There have been things in my life that have not made sense to me, and some people don't believe it when I tell them, but I promise it's true.

I do remember being a baby.

I cried a lot and my parents just thought that I was spoiled, but when they would lay me down in my bed, I remember thinking, "I can't breathe".

When I would cry, they would pick me up and I would be able to breathe without any problems. I was afraid.

My dad would bounce me up and down and he just thought that he spoiled me.

What other defense does a baby or a non-verbal have except to make sounds or to cry, and I feel for Dale who understands everything you say, but can only respond with noises that he is trying to make into words.

85

Sheila Shelton

To think about this, it has also, made me sensitive to animals, which I love.

I still have problems with my breathing, but now I am able to care for myself.

I believe that I would have died if they had left me there to cry instead of picking me up.

When they would lay me down in my bed, my mom would pull the covers up right under my chin, and I would almost panic. I felt like I was being smothered and I was helpless. If they had propped me up, this would have helped so much.

One time they laid me down in my bed and my mom said, "Maybe she'll go to sleep now." I could understand what they were saying even though I couldn't respond.

When I was a little older and could sit up and walk, I was a happier baby, because I could get up when I couldn't breathe.

Thank You, Father God for helping me through the most difficult time in my life, and for allowing me to live. Help me to do Your will.

...and how from infancy, you have known the Holy Scriptures, which are able to make you wise for salvation through faith in Christ Jesus. (2nd Timothy 3:15)

Lisa's Glasses

I was talking to my sister, Lisa on the phone one day and we were talking about the Lord.

The Miracles In My Life

Lisa said that she hadn't been able to read her Bible for a couple of weeks, because she lost her glasses.

Before we hung up, she asked me to pray that she would find them.

We hung up and immediately I prayed and asked the Lord where Lisa's glasses were and the Holy Spirit said, **"They are under her bed"**.

Immediately, I called her back, but she didn't answer the phone, so I left a message on her answering machine.

She called me back shortly and she had found them!

Lisa said that before she talked to me, she told her son, Austin to pray that she would find them and the Holy Spirit told him that they were under her bed.

Austin was also, being led by the Holy Spirit.

She said that she just looked under the edge of the bed and didn't see them, but when she heard me on her answering machine, she looked further under the bed and found them.

Lord, I know that You care about every area of our lives. Some people don't seem to want to bother You, but they don't know what they are missing. Thank You for helping Lisa to find her glasses.

We Christians have the Holy Spirit inside of us and He is our helper.

Call to Me and I will answer you and tell you great and unsearchable things you do not know. (Jeremiah 33:3)

Sheila Shelton

<u>Marijuana</u>

My sister Debbie and I were saved the same night. Debbie was nine years old and I was ten. I have always believed that Jesus is our Lord and Savior, and He came in the world to die for our sins and He is the only way to Heaven.

Without Him we would all be condemned to hell and all we have to do is to believe in Jesus and to ask Him to forgive us of all our sins; and come into our hearts and save our souls. We also, need to turn from our sins.

After I grew up, I smoked marijuana twice with friends and it depressed me so bad, that I cried and I am so thankful that I never tried any other drugs.

The Bible tells us that we can make the Holy Spirit, who is inside every believer, sad.

People tend to think that marijuana cannot harm you, but it does shrink the brain cells, not to mention what it does to the lungs.

Our lives are supposed to be filled with the Holy Spirit, not drugs.

It is a sin to do anything that damages the human body that our Lord created.

People are going to nursing homes younger these days, because drugs are destroying their lives and minds.

Thank You, Lord for not letting me enjoy this drug, because all I need is You. I know that drugs are of the devil and I just want to live for You. Drugs are a replacement of You, and are demonic.

And do not grieve the Holy Spirit of God, with whom you were sealed for the day of Redemption. (Ephesians 4;30)

Miss You

Whenever my family and I have a special dinner at my parent's house, in Potts Camp, Mississippi, I say the blessing, thanking the Lord for our food and for our precious family.

Most of my family is there for Easter, Mothers' Day, Fathers' Day, Thanksgiving, and Christmas. There are usually about thirty of us and we always have such a special time.

One time, I had just finished praying and the Holy Spirit said, **"These people are going to miss you when you are gone."**

I don't understand exactly what this means or of God's timing, but I do trust You, Lord.

I love Dale, Pete, my family and friends with all my heart and I am ready to go, but I would like to stay with them a little while longer, but the Lord knows what is best for me. I also, know that I still have work to do for You

I can't imagine how awesome it will be in Heaven with Jesus for eternity! And I know that He has work for me to do there, too.

Thank You, Father God for all Your awesome blessings and our love for each other. Thank You for giving us these special times together. But most of all, thank You for Your precious Son, Jesus.

Sheila Shelton

I will not die, but live and will proclaim what the Lord has done. (Psalm 18:17)

My Dream

Over the years I have questioned the Lord; and asked Him why my son, Dale Wilson had to be mentally handicapped.

For years, I thought that the Lord didn't love Dale and me, but I now realize that I was wrong.

One night, I had a dream that two rather wild boys came by to pick up Dale and I was so worried.

In my dreams, the Lord said, that if Dale had been normal, this is the way it would have been.

At least, I now know that Dale has a straight road to Heaven and I wouldn't want it any other way.

Thank You, Lord for taking such good care of my precious son, Dale, Pete and me. You know better, because You can see the whole picture. You are truly an amazing God and I love You!

...and last of all He (Jesus) appeared to me (Paul) also, as to one abnormally born. (1st Corinthians 15:8)

My Driveway

On December 8, 2006, a water main broke in the road in front of my house, next to my driveway and water flooded my yard, and all the adjoining yards.

The Miracles In My Life

It took Memphis, Light, Gas and Water (MLGW) awhile to get there and to get it shut off. They worked all day on it.

Before they could get the water shut off, mud started coming up out of the ground. It covered my driveway, the walk in front of my house; and my front and back yard, leaving mud about four inches deep. It was horrible!

Water covered the adjoining yards and was even in the road behind my house. The MLGW worker told me that they would pay for any damages done to my property.

During the meantime, I was in the garage, trying to sweep the water out so that it wouldn't come into the house.

It liked about an inch of coming in.

Finally, about ten-thirty that night, workers had the water back on and they left a little after midnight.

When Pete came up to pick me up for church, I had to put garbage bags on each leg and walk to the end of the driveway where he was waiting in his truck. Then I would take the bags off before I got into his truck.

When we returned home, I'd put the same garbage bags on so that I could walk back to my house, and I'd do the same thing when I'd walk to the garbage can or go to the mailbox.

I had taken such pride in my yard, having my yard sprayed seven times a year so that I would have pretty grass and pretty flower beds, and now they were destroyed.

A few days later, the men at MLGW did send a front end loader and five men to clean up the mud, rocks and brick that came out of the ground, on my driveway, my garage, my walk and my patio. But I still had a mess in my yard.

Over time, I still had to pick up rocks and brick out of my yard.

My driveway bulked up and started caving in and MLGW refused to repair it.

I prayed about this situation and put it in the Lord's hands.

My driveway got so bad that my car would sometimes drag when I was pulling in or out of the driveway, and I lived on a very busy street.

For six years, I called, wrote letters, had an attorney write a letter to claims, had a meeting with MLGW, and finally after seven years, a man came to my front door one morning and said that they were going to repair my driveway.

I got down on my knees and thanked the Lord, because He sure is a great God!

Give thanks to the Lord and proclaim His greatness. Let the whole world know what He has done. (Psalm 105:1)

My Grandfather Is In Heaven

One day, I was sitting in my recliner with my legs propped up, watching Sid Roth, a Christian Jew on

The Miracles In My Life

television (It's Supernatural), and he had a guest on his show.

I had been praying and asking the Lord if my Granddaddy Rhea was in Heaven, and I asked the Lord to please let me know.

The guest speaker stopped and said that there is someone out there who wants to know if a certain person is in Heaven, and God wants you to know that they are in Heaven.

He said, "You are sitting there in a recliner with your legs propped up and your hand is on your shoulder". He was talking to me!

Thank You, Lord for your awesome knowledge and encouragement.

…who satisfies your desires with good things so that your youth is renewed like the Eagles. (Psalm 103:5)

My Temper

I used to have a bad temper and I would get upset and throw a fit.

I had been hurt so much in my lifetime, and I was so tired of all the pain in my heart.

One time, I was praying and I asked the Lord to show me what I was doing wrong. I couldn't imagine me doing anything wrong.

I was watching the minister, Charles Stanley (In Touch Ministries) as he preached on Christian television one day, and all of a sudden he stopped and said, **"And stop throwing those fits!"**

Sheila Shelton

I knew that it was a word from the Lord meant for me; and it really did have my attention.

Now, my attitude has changed drastically.

To God be the glory.

For our struggle is not against flesh and blood, but against the rulers, against the authorities, against the powers of this dark world and against the spiritual forces of evil in the heavenly realms. (Ephesians 6:12)

Thoughts of Suicide

When I was growing up, I was extremely depressed and I thought about suicide a lot, even though I was a Christian and I was always sad.

Looking back, I realize that I should have been on medication.

A few years ago, I was crying and I cannot explain the emptiness and loneliness that I felt, but it was a horrible feeling and I just prayed to die.

I got my gun out, while I cried until I couldn't cry any more.

I just felt so alone and my nearest family member was Dale, my only child, who was in Arlington Developmental Center at the time. I just felt so alone, so empty.

Deep down, I knew that I couldn't commit suicide, because I knew that my autistic, non-verbal son needed me so much.

I cried and prayed, and it just seemed like everything had gone wrong in my life.

The Miracles In My Life

The Holy Spirit told me to get up and take my last nerve bill that I had saved, and to get some sleep.

I went to sleep on the couch with my gun on my chest and when I woke up, I felt so much better. I had a peaceful sleep and the Lord comforted me.

I shared this story with one of my friends in my singles Bible Study at church, and she told me about her sister who had tried to commit suicide several times, but always called someone at the last minute.

The sister, who was also, in my Bible study said that she would take a bunch of pills, get scared and call her aunt or her sister.

The last time she tried to commit suicide she had made up her mind that she wasn't going to call for help this time.

She took a shower, put her makeup on, and took a handful of pills, and went to bed.

The next morning she actually woke up and everything in her apartment was torn up, even her plants were out of their pots.

There had been spiritual warfare in her apartment that night and the holy angels had won that battle, because people were praying for her.

We just can't imagine how powerful our prayers are.

The preacher, Charles Stanley said that "Anxiety becomes sin when we don't deal with it in the proper fashion. It has a negative effect on every area of your life. It is like poison and we need to bring it to God in prayer in the Spirit of Thanksgiving."

He also, says that we don't have to live in anxiety unless we choose to and how long you keep it is the key. It can have a devastating effect on your health. Anxiety clears up and physical problems clear up, too, and I refuse to live this way anymore.

Brother Stanley also, said that we need to read: **Rejoice in the heart always. I will say it again: Rejoice! Let your gentleness be evident to all. The Lord is near. Do not be anxious about anything, but in everything, by prayer and petition, with thanksgiving, present your requests to God. And the peace of God, which transcends all understanding, will guard your hearts and your minds in Christ Jesus. (Philippians 4:4-7)**

The Lord has all the answers. We just need to totally learn to depend on Him, read our Bibles daily, pray and talk to Him, and praise Him all during the day and night. Be bold in the Lord. Look what I overcame with His help.

Tell the Lord that you put all your anxiety in His hands and watch Him work. This is one of the benefits of being a Christian. Don't let the devil win. He only has power if you allow him to.

Thank You, Lord, for the power of prayer and that I don't have to live depressed anymore.

The thief comes only to steal and kill and destroy; I have come that they may have life; and have it to the full. (John 10:10)

My Thought Life

Two different times this has happened to me and I don't really understand it.

I was home both days and all day long had reoccurring bad thoughts coming to my mind, but I would not let myself get upset.

These were thoughts about different things that had happened to me, and also, about people who had hurt me in my lifetime.

All these different circumstances kept coming to my mind, but I never got upset.

I know that the battlefield is in the mind, and the Bible tells us to renew our minds, and refuse to think about these things.

All my life, I would just be devastated by all these terrible thoughts, but not now.

I thought about what the Bible says about the fiery darts of the enemy, and I knew it was the devil trying to attack me.

All of a sudden, it was like, "Ok, you win. You can't be defeated" and I had the best feeling. The devil had attacked me and I had won.

Thank You, Lord that I have power over the devil in my mind, and I don't have to think about the evil things he puts in my mind. I refuse to listen to him and be defeated.

I will change what I am thinking about and only think about good things. I will renew my mind and I will refuse to be defeated anymore.

Sheila Shelton

Submit yourselves to God. Resist the devil and he will flee from you. (James 4:7)

Only Flesh

Before Pete and I married, he lived in the country and had hunting dogs that he kept in a pen. Otherwise, they would run off and possibly get killed.

They were half Running Walker and half Beagles, and I just loved them.

When I would go down there to see him, he'd let his four dogs out to get exercise, and they would follow me everywhere, while I rode his ATV four-wheeler, and I enjoyed this so much!

I would ride the four-wheeler to the little pond and they would run and jump in the water, play, get a drink, and when they were refreshed, they would be ready to go again.

I would stop and let them play, but when I'd crack up the four-wheeler, they would come running. They loved it and so did I.

One day, I was riding on a trail through the woods like I always did, and I hit a stump.

Pete had put a windshield on his four-wheeler, and when I hit the stump, it jerked the front wheel around and my head hit the edge of the windshield between my eyes, causing a gash.

Blood was everywhere, even on my shoes and I needed stitches, even though I refused to go to the Emergency Room.

The Miracles In My Life

I thought my nose was broken, because it was numb, but it was only bruised.

The Holy Spirit said, **"It's only flesh"** and somehow this seemed to make me feel better.

I couldn't get Pete on the phone, because he was plowing in a field; and couldn't hear his cell phone, so I had to walk to where he was and all four of the sweet little dogs followed me. It sure did scare him when he saw me, covered in blood.

Pete cleaned me up and put a band aid on my forehead until I could purchase a butterfly band aid to hold the incision together.

Thank You, Lord for comforting me when I was wounded, and for allowing us to enjoy your precious animals. They need to be with people who love them.

No, in all these things we are more than conquerors through Him who loved us. (Romans 8:37)

Pete's Four -Wheeler

One time Pete asked me to go with him to his deer camp to get his three deer stands.

He told me to stay by his truck, because everything had grown up and it was snaky where his deer stands were.

He would ride his four-wheeler to each one, take them down, and pull them back to his truck.

On his way back with one of the deer stands, he turned the four-wheeler over backwards and he started calling me so I could go where he was.

Sheila Shelton

If he had gotten off, the four-wheeler would have possibly turned over on him and he could have been seriously injured. He was trapped.

I pulled on the front, even picking my feet up off the ground, but I couldn't budge it.

So, I prayed and asked the Lord to help me. Then, I tried again and the front came down with Pete on it. This was not my strength!

Thank You Lord, for Your great power and strength!

…and His incomparable great power for us who believe. That is like the working of His mighty strength. (Ephesians 1:19)

Plan of Salvations on Airplanes

I worked for a major airline for twenty-five years, and after we unloaded the airplanes and the people were off, I would go upstairs and take four or five copies of the Plan of Salvation with me.

I would pray and ask the Holy Spirit to tell me where to place each paper and would start at the front of the airplane and work my way to the back.

When the Holy Spirit was ready for me to stop, He would turn my whole body in the direction that He wanted me to go and direct my hand to what seat back pocket He wanted me to put the Plan of Salvation in.

This happened several times over the years.

The Bible tells us that His word will not return void, and I would claim that scripture and pray for

The Miracles In My Life

the salvation of the person who found it, and I also, prayed that they would lead others to the Lord.

Thank You, Lord for Your awesome plan of Salvation!

...so is My word that goes out from My mouth. It will not return empty, but will accomplish what I desire and achieve the purpose for which it was sent. (Isaiah 55:11)

Rotator Cuff Tear

In May 2009, while working alone in the bag room at work, I received a full rotator cuff tear to my right shoulder.

My doctor said that it was torn in half and sticking up, like the hood of a car.

The ticket counter at the airport would send bags down to me in the bag room below on a conveyor belt, and I would take them off and put them on the correct cart, to go to the airplane.

Each cart held approximately fifty bags and sometimes, I would be loading six carts at a time.

Then, I would mark the correct destination on a computer generated worksheet.

It was a two man job and I repeatedly asked for help and the union also, tried to get me the help that I needed. It was a tough job for a woman and I didn't get breaks, just a thirty minute lunch break.

The boss was told to get me some help, but he refused.

After 911, we were working with a skeleton crew.

Sheila Shelton

In the bag room, the flight would close out several minutes before departure and I would give the worksheet to the crew chief, and he would know how to load the airplanes with the appropriate weight.

Sometimes, we had basketball, baseball, football, and bowling teams, with their heavy equipment, and sometimes we had musical bands, but it was job security for us and we appreciated the business.

Some of the bags would weigh over a hundred pounds and the electric wheelchairs were extremely heavy.

We were fortunate enough to be able to load animals, which everyone loved, especially the puppies.

In twenty-five years, I was trained to do all the jobs, including dumping lavatories on airplanes, putting water on them, fueling airplanes, fueling equipment, loading and unloading, cleaning, pushing the aircraft out, de-icing and anti-icing, fill in when a crew chief was off or on vacation, and now I was working in the bag room.

For a while, I worked at American Airlines Cargo, doing both the office work and the dock work, and sometimes this was a very stressful job.

They closed the cargo facility, even though it was doing a booming business and I had to go back to loading and unloading the airplanes.

Basically, I enjoyed my work and have always loved airplanes.

The Miracles In My Life

After my right rotator cuff was torn in half, the doctor told me that I wouldn't be able to do the job anymore, that I would re-injure my right shoulder, so he placed me on a forty pound weight restriction on my lifting.

When I took the paperwork to my boss, he told me that he did not have anything for me.

I feel like, if I had the help that I had needed, I would not have had a full rotator cuff tear, nor would I have had to have a pin inserted in my shoulder.

To this very day, it still bothers my shoulder when I vacuum my house and do light housework.

The union said that it was negligence and I agree.

That was a strange feeling, after I had worked at a steady job for twenty-five years, to have someone tell me that they don't have anything for me.

I do miss being around the airplanes and most of the people I worked with, but I do not miss the hard work, nor do I miss working in the bad weather.

This job used to be a career job, but things have really changed. It sure did hurt, but I did retire from the airline on December 1, 2012.

The Lord might have given me this time that I was off work to write my book. He works in mysterious ways.

Review the past for Me, let us argue the matter together; state the cause of your innocence. (Isaiah 43:26)

Sheila Shelton

__Singing To The Lord__

Every night before I go to bed, I read my Bible, say my prayer, and walk through the house singing, and praising the Lord.

One night it was getting late and I was on the computer and I thought, "I need to get ready for bed".

The Holy Spirit said that He was waiting on me to sing to Him, and I thought, "Wow!"

I have never thought about the Lord being my audience when I sing praises to Him, but I know that He is.

The Lord tells us to make a joyful noise to Him.

I can't sing, but the noise I made to my Father that night…and every night, is really joyful, and comes from my heart.

I can always feel the Holy Spirit so strong, and sometimes it feels as if the Lord puts His hand on the back of my neck.

I have put my hand up there to brush whatever it was away, and it was nothing there.

Thank You, Lord for Your awesome presence!

Let the Word of Christ dwell in you richly as you teach and admonish one another with all wisdom, and as you sing psalm, hymns and spiritual songs with gratitude in your hearts to God. (Colossians 3:16)

__Speaking In Tongues__

Every night after I read my Bible and before I say my prayer, I walk through the house praising

The Miracles In My Life

the Lord, as I stated before. This is why we were created, to worship and praise the Lord.

I have always wanted to speak in tongues, one of the gifts given to us by the Holy Spirit, so I had prayed and asked the Lord to give me the gift.

One day when I was off work, I was on the computer and all of a sudden, for no reason, the tie back on the curtain fell, releasing the curtain.

I said, "Ok, Lord. What do You want me to do," and the Lord said, **"Start praising Me"**, so I got up and started walking around the house, praising the Lord.

I remember the song, "When the praises go up, the glory comes down, where sin used to dwell, grace now abounds. There's healing and hope and love all around, when the praises go up, the glory comes down...." I began to sing it.

I walked through the kitchen, through the dining room, the hall, the living room and back through the kitchen, while I was praising the Lord.

Then my words became jumbled, and I started speaking in tongues, and kept it up for about two hours and it was awesome! I felt so close to the Lord and nothing feels better than that.

Afterwards, I could speak in tongues anytime I wanted.

Tongues, then, are a sign, nor for the believers, but for the unbelievers; prophesy, however is for believers, not for unbelievers. (1ˢᵗ Corinthians 14:22)

Sheila Shelton

The Abby

Several years ago, when my son was little, several friends invited me to meet them at a club in Oxford, Mississippi, called The Abby.

I was lonely so I decided to go a couple of times.

I didn't like the hard rock music the band was playing, but I did enjoy talking to my friends.

While I was there, the Holy Spirit kept repeating over and over, **"You've got Dale. You've got Dale."**

I could feel the demons in that place so strong, so I had to leave. It was almost unbearable.

Father, I don't know what all was going on in The Abby, but I do know that You wanted me to leave for my own good and I obeyed. I thank You, Lord.

I know your deeds. See, I have placed before you an open door that no one can shut. I know that you have little strength, yet you have kept My word and have not denied My (Jesus) name. (Revelations 3:8)

The Best Job

We moved to Memphis, Tennessee in 1984, and I kept working at Wurlitzer Piano Company in Holly Springs, Mississippi, where I had worked for eleven years.

As I stated earlier, I was driving about forty miles one way every day, married at the time to my sec-

The Miracles In My Life

ond husband, and had Dale by my first husband, Ricky who left when he was a baby.

I was only making five dollars and six cents an hour; and paying someone fifty dollars a week just to put Dale on the school bus in the mornings.

Expecting to be able to draw unemployment from the state of Mississippi, I quit work, but the state of Mississippi would not help me, because they said I did not quit for a good reason.

Back then, I didn't know anyone who could keep Dale when school was out, and I didn't know what to do.

The child care centers in Memphis would not keep a mentally-handicapped child, because they didn't have nurses.

I felt like I hit a closed door everywhere I went and it seemed like everything was coming against Dale and me.

My husband was a truck driver so we didn't have medical insurance, and Dale took medication for seizures.

I applied at Memphis City School for a typing job, and at one time, I could type about eighty words a minute, but I failed the typing test. I just could not understand why, so I prayed and asked the Lord if it was His will to give me the job. I was so upset about not passing the test.

Memphis City Schools required that you be able to type thirty words a minute, which is not bad.

Sheila Shelton

So, I went back and took the test again and failed it, and I realized that this was not where the Lord wanted me to be. I was at peace.

About two weeks later, American Airlines called me and I was hired May 25, 1985, as a Fleet Service Clerk, making more money.

I would have health insurance and also, travel benefits!

This was the best job I ever had and I thank You, Lord for placing me exactly where You wanted me to be. You are an awesome God with wonderful plans for me, and I realize that I just have to pray and wait on you.

I have always loved airplanes and being around them, and this was a desire of my heart, and an exciting job.

And we know that in all things God works for the good of those who love Him, who have been called according to His purpose. (Romans 8:28)

The Blow Out

I was traveling from Memphis, Tennessee to Baldwin, Mississippi where my sister, Freda lived, to help her take care of some business.

While I was driving down Highway seventy-eight, the Holy Spirit said to me two or three times that I was going to have a blowout.

The speed limit was seventy miles per hour, which I was driving, when I had a blowout on my right front tire.

The Miracles In My Life

I slowed down and almost came to a stop, before I pulled over on the side of the road. I knew that I could flip the car if I pulled over too quickly.

I remembered hearing about a family who was killed when they had a blow-out on the interstate; and had pulled over too quickly.

Having trouble getting the lug nuts off the tire, I prayed and asked the Lord to help me.

A van pulled over and a man traveling through the area changed the tire for me.

Lord, Thank You for warning us and protecting us in every situation.

"Have I not commanded you? Be strong and courageous. Do not be terrified, do not be discouraged, for the Lord you God will be with you wherever you go." (Joshua 1:9)

The Book of Daniel

I have read the Bible several times and have always marked what I read, so one day, I was looking through the Bible to make sure I hadn't missed anything.

This reading is besides my other daily Bible reading and when I got to the book of Daniel, I prayed and asked the Lord if He wanted me to read this book again, since I had already read it several times.

On Saturday night, Pete and I went to church and Brother Arnold was preaching. He said, **"And**

you really do need to read the book of Daniel", and I knew that it was a word from the Lord.

I did reread the book and received such a blessing.

Thank You, Father God for giving me clear direction, in Jesus name.

Those who are wise will shine like the brightness of the heavens, and those who lead many to righteousness, like the stars for ever and ever. (Daniel 12:3)

The Cell Phone

I joined ATC-Fitness Center where I work out, and one day, I had a couple of things in my hand, and I dropped my cell phone on the floor and the flap came open. I put it back together, but I could not turn the cell phone on.

So, I prayed and asked the Lord to help me.

After I dropped the phone, I kept feeling like I needed to go back where I had dropped it, so I went back to the area, but there was nothing there.

Finally, I just put the phone in the Lord's hands and knew that everything would be alright.

Pete always wanted me to call him when I arrived anywhere, when I left and then again when I arrived home, because he always wants to make sure that I am safe. Also, my car had a lot of miles on it and he made sure that I didn't break down. I appreciate it, too.

The Miracles In My Life

He also, puts his hand on my car and prays that the Lord will keep my car and me safe.

I asked the man at the desk if I could borrow his phone to call Pete and tell him what had happened.

I opened the flap and showed him, and felt so silly when he gave me the battery that had fallen out of my phone. Someone had turned it in and I was so embarrassed, not realizing that my battery had fallen out.

Lord, thank You for letting me get my battery back and my phone working on this day; and please let me be more sensitive to the Holy Spirit's leading.

For nothing is impossible with God. (Luke 1:27)

The Freezer

My parents had a chest freezer that was about forty years old, and my dad was getting worried about the cord on the freezer being dangerous.

Several nights before I went to sleep, I would be lying in bed, and I would feel the Holy Spirit urging me to pray about the freezer and my parents' safety, which I did.

When I talked to my mom about the freezer, she said that she had felt the same way I did and she would also, pray.

Finally, they purchased a new freezer and when my dad unplugged the old one, he could tell that the cord had caught on fire. Wonder who put it out?

Father, God, thank You for protecting our homes and vehicles, too. You are such a good and loving God. You never cease to amaze me.

For He will command His angels concerning you to guard you in all your ways. (Psalms 91:11)

The Money

I was on an unpaid leave of absence from work; and was having some financial problems.

I prayed about my situation and told the Lord that I put my financial problems in His hands. I didn't know what He was going to do, but I did trust Him.

As I looked in the computer on the American Airlines' Jetnet website, which always showed a copy of my paychecks, I looked under vacation pay, but really, I thought I had received it all.

It showed that they still owed me for two-hundred hours of vacation pay, so I emailed my boss and he responded that he would check on it.

The next day, I received an email from him, saying that they did owe me and they also, found an additional two-hundred hours, making it a total of four-hundred hours!

I was so proud of that money that I was able to pay the taxes on my house and to catch up on all my bills.

Lord, You are such a great God and I know that you are concerned about every area of my life. I just have to ask You and believe that you will take care of the situation.

And to Him who is able to do immeasurable more than we can ask or imagine, according to His great power that is at work within us. (Ephesians 3:20)

The Presence

As I stated before, Dale Wilson, my son started having seizures when he was a day old, caused by forceps during birth. A C-section would have prevented this.

He is very fragile and we have to keep him away from caffeine and the spice, "Sage".

His seizures are mostly controlled by medication.

When Dale was about thirteen years old, he had a bad seizure, so I took him to the doctor and had him checked out, and after we made sure he was alright, the doctor sent us home. We were always so alone.

He was so weak that I had to feed him and would pick him up and take him to the bathroom.

One of the times I took him to the bathroom, I picked him up, wrapped his long, thin legs around my waist, but they still almost hung down to the floor.

When I walked out of the bathroom, I felt a great "presence" and I knew they we were being watched, and they were talking about us.

Sheila Shelton

I felt pure joy and it was such an awesome feeling that I will never forget.

Thank You, Lord for Your great presence, and for loving on Dale and me when we need it so bad. We would have been so alone if we hadn't have had You.

Therefore, since we are surrounded by such a great cloud of witnesses, let us throw off everything that so easily entangles, and let us run with perseverance the race marked out for us. (Hebrews 12:1)

The Shaking Bed

My mom told me that her bed would sometimes shake when her and my dad were in it, and she didn't know why.

I went into their bedroom, praised the Lord, and demanded every unclean spirit that was in their bedroom and in their house, to go back to the pit (hell), in Jesus name. They had to go, because of the power of the Lord's name.

Later, I asked my mom if it had ever happened again and she said, "No".

Lord, thank You for giving us Christians Your power, because we have the Holy Spirit living inside of us.

"The name of the Lord is a strong tower; the righteous run to it and is safe." (Proverbs 8:10)

The Shoes

For a few months, I had seen a commercial on television, and at the end of it, they would show a

The Miracles In My Life

woman with the prettiest red shoes on, that I had ever seen. I love shoes!

One day, I was watching television with Pete's mom and I saw the commercial again.

I didn't even know what the commercial was even about, but I saw one word and wrote it down.

When Pete came into the house, I told him about the shoes and he typed the name of the commercial in Google search on his computer, but it didn't show anything.

Pete then pulled up eBay and typed in RED SHOES, and it pulled up about thirty-thousand pairs of pretty red shoes, and I looked through a lot of them, but I didn't find the shoes that I had seen on the commercial.

I prayed, "Lord, if you want me to have those shoes, I know that you will give them to me".

The next day, Judy Parker and I went to see our sons, Dale and his housemate, Charlie Parker, like we do every week when we spend the day with them.

This particular day, we drove them to Covington, Tennessee and back.

Pete called and wanted to know where we were and when we would be back, and I told him about four-thirty or five o'clock to our sons' group home.

He asked me what size shoes I wore and I told him six and a half, or a seven, but I didn't think that I could wear a larger size.

Sheila Shelton

He wanted me to meet him in Memphis at a shoe store called, Cook and Love, and for me to ask to see Evelyn, which I did.

She brought out a pair of red shoes that I had seen on the commercial; and they only had one pair left and they were a size seven and a half, but they fit perfectly, so Pete came into the store and paid for the shoes, for my birthday. I was so excited!

That morning, on his computer, he had asked Google what the name of the shoes were on that commercial and someone had answered him!

He looked for the shoes at Macy's and Dillard's, but could not find them in the Memphis area, so he went back to the computer to Google, and asked where he could find the shoes. The computer told him that the Cook and Love Shoe Store had them.

He called the store and they only had one red pair left, a size seven and a half, and they actually fit!

Now, my feet have actually grown and I do wear a size seven or a seven and a half.

I loved my shoes so much and was so proud of them. I would wear them, take them off when I got home; and put them on a paper towel on my dresser, and I kept admiring them.

One day the Holy Spirit asked me if the shoes were an idol to me and I said, "No, Lord".

I gook the shoes off the dresser and put them back in the closet. But, I do enjoy wearing them frequently.

The Miracles In My Life

Thank You, Lord for giving me the desires of my heart; and for caring about my wants and needs. You are such a great God!

Delight yourself in the Lord and He will give you the desires of your heart. (Psalm 37:4)

The Van In My House

One day I left for work and had been gone about an hour and a half, when my boss came to get me and said that someone ran into my garage door.

I thought, "Oh no. Not my garage door. It took me forever to get it."

I left and went home to see what damage had been done.

When I neared my house, I saw the fire department, an ambulance and a lot of people were at my house, and in my yard.

I looked at my garage door and it was fine, and I breathed a sign of relief. Then, I looked at the front of my house and a van was sticking out of the house where a wall used to be. I just couldn't believe it!

Someone had lost control of their vehicle on the street after a car ran into them, and the man drove into my living room, but he didn't have any insurance.

I felt sorry for the man, because I knew that he was hurt, but he refused to be transported to the

Sheila Shelton

hospital by ambulance, because he didn't have any insurance.

But I realized that this is only material things and I did not let myself get upset. I wanted to have a major pity party and ask the Lord why He allowed this to happen. I grew up feeling sorry for myself, and I refused to be defeated by the devil again. He just kept trying to destroy me.

The man driving the van couldn't speak English so the police department sent a Spanish speaking officer to question him.

My insurance man was in Nashville, Tennessee at a meeting so I had to sit in the garage all day waiting on the insurance people to send someone to board up my living room wall. It was Summer time and the weather was scorching hot. I felt so alone!

In the living room, my stereo had been destroyed, my big screen television demolished and I don't remember what all was destroyed, and it was a mess.

About a week later, my insurance company started sending people to repair my house, which took quite some time, but I stayed in it every night, even when they were working on it.

I was so thankful to finally have my house back to normal and I was able to pay it off with money that I received from the insurance company for some of the contents of my house. This was another answer to my prayer!

The Miracles In My Life

Your eyes saw my unformed body. All the days ordained for me were written in Your (the Lord's) book before one of them came to be. (Psalm 139:16)

The Water Leak

I had a water leak by the sidewalk in my yard, and my water bill was around forty dollars a month. It usually ran about ten dollars so I knew something was wrong.

I called Memphis, Light, Gas and Water (MLGW); and they said that the water leak was on my side, making it my responsibility.

Pete took his shovel and dug down by the sidewalk, and found where the leak was, so he cut the piece of pipe out that had a hole in it, and purchased the parts to repair it.

When he was trying to repair it, I was praying that the Lord would help him. It was already dark outside and I had to hold the flashlight for him to see.

He was trying to hook the two pieces of pipe together, it was in a tight space, and he was having a hard time screwing the two pieces together, so he stopped and rested. There was only room for one hand in the hole.

I prayed and the Lord told me to try it. I started to pull my hand from the hole, and the Lord told me to try it again, so I did. The Lord showed me that the pipe would have to be picked up on one

Sheila Shelton

end to get the threads even before they could be screwed together, and I told Pete.

I was not strong enough to do it with one hand so Pete tried it and it worked.

Lord thank You for sending someone to help me in my time of need and for helping us to solve the problem. You care about everything that concerns us. You are such a great God, and I love You!

So, do not fear for I am with you; do not be dismayed for I am your God. I will strengthen you and help you. I will uphold you with My righteous right hand. (Isaiah 41:10)

The Wind

Several years ago my son, Dale and I lived in a trailer house when he was little.

One night the weather was getting bad so my mom called to see if Dale and I wanted to come to her house, but we were already in bed.

They lived about a half a mile away, but it was already raining, and the wind was blowing hard so we stayed home.

In the Bible, I remembered Jesus commanded the wind to stop blowing, and it obeyed.

So, I prayed and commanded the wind to stop blowing, in Jesus' name, and it did!

Lord, You never cease to amaze me and I realize that You are everything that I need. Thank You, Lord!

The Miracles In My Life

Now faith is being sure of what we hope for and certain of what we do not see. (Hebrews 11:1)

The Wreck

It seems like the devil has tried to destroy everything that I have.

One day I went to Pete's deer camp and rode around with him all day; and before I left to go home, we went to Harmon's Restaurant to eat fish. It was dark when I left to go home.

We didn't see a deer all day and I was wishing that I would see one on the way home.

Pete told me to be sure I didn't speed going home or I might get a ticket, so I made sure I drove the speed limit of fifty-five miles per hour.

I was driving down the road when a deer ran across the road in front of me from the left to the right side of the road, and ran off into the woods.

Then, I looked to the left and two more deer were coming straight towards my car.

The one in front turned, trying to miss my car and hit the left front side of my car like a football player, and I screamed.

By the time I came to a stop, I was in a valley between two hills, and a woman pulled up behind me and got out of her car to make sure I was alright. I was badly shaken and couldn't get the driver door of my car to open.

I wanted to call Pete, but the woman told me that I would not be able to use my cell phone until

Sheila Shelton

I drove to the top of the next hill to call him. I was afraid that he wouldn't be in a serviceable area, where my cell phone would be able to reach him.

Mississippi has a lot of dead places for cell phone users, and it is rather inconvenient.

But thank the Lord I did reach him, and met him back at the restaurant where we had eaten earlier.

My left headlight had been broken out when the deer hit the car, and the left side of my car looked awful.

Pete had to pull the fender out to keep it from rubbing the tire, and remove the head light which had broken glass everywhere.

I had a major pity party, and I cried and remembered everything bad that has ever happened to me.

Pete followed me all the way back home that evening, then drove back to his deer camp.

The car was totaled so I purchased it back from the insurance company, and had someone to repair it. I could not afford car payments.

After the car was repaired, I had to get a Salvage Title to be able to drive it.

Deer do millions of dollars of damage a year. They eat crops, vegetable gardens and also, damage a lot of vehicles who hit them or who they hit. It's a major problem.

Pete planted a patch of peas this year and the deer ate every one of them. We were so disappointed.

The Miracles In My Life

Lord, thank You for keeping me safe in yet another bad situation.

My mouth will speak in praise of the Lord. Let every creature praise His holy name forever and ever. (Psalm 145:21)

Trust Me

Like I had said before, I had to put my son, Dale in Arlington Developmental Center (ADC), for his own safety; and he stayed there for a total of ten years.

I know that I am repeating myself sometimes, but I am just trying to stress what the Lord did for Dale and me.

I've had hard times in my life, but putting him in ADC was the hardest thing I had to do.

Thank the Lord, the medical staff monitored his medication and took him off some of it, and the first week, he was completely different.

Dr. Jones said that Dale was on so much medication that he didn't even know what he was doing.

I can't understand why a perfectly normal person would even try drugs, because it is demonic (sorcery), and in **Revelations 21:8** and other books of the Holy Bible, it talks about this.

The devil is trying to destroy their souls and bodies, and they are sold out to him.

People who are mentally and physically handicapped would do anything to be able to have a healthy mind and body.

Sheila Shelton

I was finally working full-time after thirteen years, but was devastated when my place of employment demoted me and others to part-time again.

When my boss told me, I couldn't help but cry, and I asked the Lord why He had allowed this to happen, and He said, **"Trust Me"**.

A short time later, ADC started placing their patients into group homes in the community, and I was asked if I wanted Dale to be placed in one, and I willingly agreed.

I helped with the decisions of the two individuals who I wanted to be Dale's housemates, finding the right home, purchasing furniture, and everything they needed from furniture to sheets.

It was an exciting time and a very busy one.

If I had been working full-time, it would have been impossible to help with all these details in my precious son's life, and I was enjoying myself so much.

I am very involved in Dale's life and I met nurses, picked out his new PCP, and met his new dietician, an advocate, behavior analysts, and all sorts of people who would be

involved in Dale and his two housemates, Charlie and Jeff's lives.

I had to work with an Individual Support Plan (ISP)

Coordinator and an advocate to help plan Dale's life for the entire year.

The Miracles In My Life

I'm not only his mom, I'm his legal guarding, because Dale is considered incapacitated, mentally unable to make decisions for himself.

This had been a busy, but rewarding year and I wouldn't

change it for anything.

After all this was over, I was promoted back to full-time

work again.

The Lord told me to trust Him and He always has an awesome plan for our lives.

Thankfully, the group home has been successful with

wonderful caretakers who care for them twenty-four hours

a day, seven days a week.

I believe that the Lord will bless these caretakers and their families, because of what they do for our sons. The Bible says that what we do for others, He will do for us. That is a Bible promise.

The caretakers take Dale, Charlie and Jeff to all their

doctors' appointments, and they have an activity Calendar,

that the house manager creates on a monthly basis.

It is unbelievable all the activities that they get to participate in from bowling, movies, museums, trips to the park, walking on the river, libraries, church, to the mall, out to eat, arts and crafts, and shopping, to mention a few. Judy and I visit them

Sheila Shelton

one day a week, usually on Friday, and spend quality time with them.

Dale wants to learn to read and write, and he loves his ABC puzzles.

I spell different words for him, and he is so interested in learning.

Thank You, Lord for taking such good care of our boys.

"Do not let your hearts be troubled. Trust in God. Trust also, in Me (Jesus)." (John 14:1)

Virginia Technical College

A few years ago, my parents and I went to Bluefield, Virginia to visit my aunt and uncle.

One day my mom, my aunt, her daughter and grandchildren, and I went shopping, and rode around to see the sights.

We drove through a pretty little town called Blackburg, Virginia, and drove past Virginia Technical College.

The Holy Spirit told me that I was going to hear more about this school later,

A couple of weeks after we got home, I heard that a student had killed several other students in a horrible massacre.

Father God, thank You for Your protection and the knowledge You give us. Please teach us to pray for every situation before it unfolds, in Jesus name.

There is not a righteous man on earth who does what is right and never sins. (Ecclesiastes 17:20)

My Friend and Sister-In-Law

My dear friend, and sister-in-law, Vivian called and asked me to go to J C Penney's with her to purchase a pair of Gloria Vanderbilt jeans that she had been wanting.

When we arrived, Penney's was out of what she wanted so she settled for a different brand.

A few days later, it was her birthday, and her husband took her out to eat, and offered to stop by a different Penney's store to see if they had the jeans that she wanted in her size.

Then she started looking at a different brand and she picked up a pair, and underneath was one pair of Gloria Vanderbilt jeans that she had wanted in her exact size and length, the only pair in the whole store.

It was as if the Lord had hidden a pair just for Vivian and she thanked and praised the Lord for them.

Thank You, Lord for giving Vivian the desire of her heart! You are such a great God!

Commit to the Lord whatever you do, and your plans will succeed. (Proverbs 16:3)

Was It A Dream?

I don't know if this was a dream or what, but it was so real and I have never forgotten it.

I was in darkness and the Lord came to me. He was so bright that I could not look at Him, and He told me that He was going to send me back, but it was going to be hard.

He told me that he was going to give me a handicapped child, and I said, "Lord, give me two," and He said, **"No, I don't put more on you than you can handle."**

I was so excited! I was determined to live the kind of life that the Lord wanted me to live, and to please Him in every way.

But when I look back over the years, I can see that the devil tried to destroy me, and keep me from doing the will of the Father. I had the power to fight him, but didn't know how.

Now, I realize that the Lord gave me a mentally handicapped son to draw me closer to Him. He brought me to my knees, and taught me that He is what it's all about.

I have made so many foolish mistakes, but I asked the Lord to forgive me, and to help me to live for Him. I've never been happier, because I do have the peace of God.

For He rescued us from the domain of darkness, and transferred us to the kingdom of His beloved Son (Jesus), in whom we have redemption, the forgiveness of sins. (Colossians 1:13)

Chapter 14
Salvation Bible Verses

For God so loved the world that He gave His one and only Son (Jesus), that whoever believes in Him shall not perish, but have eternal life. (John 3:16)

For it is by grace you have been saved, through faith, and this is not from yourselves, it is the gift of God, not by works, so that no one can boast. (Ephesians 2:8,9)

Now faith is being sure of what we hope for and certain of what we do not see. (Hebrews 11:1)

If we endure, we will rule with Him (Jesus). If we disown Him, He will disown us. If we are faithless, He will remain faithful, for He cannot disown Himself. (2nd Timothy 2:12,13)

Know that a man is not justified by observing the law, but by faith in Jesus Christ. So we too, have put our faith in Christ Jesus that we may be justified by faith in Christ and not by observing the law, because by observing the law, no one will be justified. (Galatians 2:16)

Sheila Shelton

And without faith it is impossible to please God, because anyone who comes to Him must believe that He exists and that He rewards those who earnestly seek Him. (Hebrews 11:6)

I (Jesus) tell you the truth. He who believes has everlasting life. (John 6:47)

Jesus answered, "I am the way and the truth and the life. No one comes to the Father except through Me. "If you really knew Me, you would know my Father as well. From now on, you do know Him and have seen Him." (John 14:6,7)

And I (Jesus) will ask the Father, and He will give you another counselor to be with you forever- the Spirit of Truth. The world cannot accept Him, because it neither sees Him nor knows Him. But you know Him, for He lives with you and will be in you. (John 14:16,17)

Pray and Receive Jesus Now

To accept Jesus as your Lord and Savior, you can pray to Him in your own words or pray: **Father God, please forgive me of all my sins-past, present and future, and come into my heart and save my soul. Thank You for sending Jesus to the cross to die for my sins. Please help me to live for You every day and to read my Bible daily, get in a good church and get baptized. Jesus, I do believe that**

The Miracles In My Life

You are the Son of God and I will praise you every day, in Jesus name, Amen.

You are saved if you pray and believe in Jesus by faith.

When we are saved, we are sealed by Jesus' Holy Spirit who lives inside of us, and He will also, be our helper.

And you also, were included in Christ when you heard the truth, the gospel of your salvation. Having believed, you were marked with a seal, the promised Holy Spirit Who is a deposit guaranteeing our inheritance until the redemption of those who are God's possession to the praise of His glory. (Ephesians 1:13, 14)

Call someone and tell them of your awesome decision to accept Jesus as your Lord and Savior.

Get in a Bible believing church where you can worship with other believers and also, make good Christian friends.

As iron sharpens iron, so one man sharpens another. (Proverbs 27:17)

Get baptized. The Lord commands us to do this. It is not a suggestion.

I would also, suggest that you read your Bible and study it every day. It sure has made a difference in my life.

Also, a Bible believing church where you can worship with other believers, and make good Christian friends is so helpful.

The Bible is God's word and it is truth. We don't want anyone to try to deceive us.

Sheila Shelton

I love on the Lord all during the day. I say, "I love you, Jesus", and He says, **"I love you, too, Sheila"!**

It is such a blessing and the Lord will bless you beyond your wildest imagination. I always praise Him before I say my prayers; and it's also a way to get prayers answered.

Atheists say there is no God. I would like to ask them, "What if you are wrong and I am right? Then you will have a lot to loose."

But I know without a doubt that there is a one God, God the Father, God the Son (Jesus), and God the Holy Spirit.

Everyone who is living is waiting to either go to Heaven to be with Jesus or to a sulfur burning Hell to live in darkness for eternity. What will you choose? To not make a decision is a decision.

For the wages of sin is death, but the gift of God is eternal life in Christ Jesus our Lord. (Romans 6:23)

Chapter 15
Salvation Is Of The Jews

Most of the Bible verses that I use in this book are from the New International Version Bible.

"You Samaritans worship what you do not know; we worship what we do know, for salvation is from the Jews." (John 4:22)

"I will bless those who bless you (the Jewish People)". (Genesis 12:3)

Therefore the Lord Himself will give you a sign: The virgin will be with child and give birth to a son, and they will call Him Immanuel. (Isaiah 7:14)

"The virgin will be with child and will give birth to a son and they will call Him Immanuel" –which means, "God with us." (Matthew 1:23)

But when the time had fully come, God sent His Son, born of a woman, born under law. (Galatians 4:4)

And we have seen and testify that the Father has sent His son to be the Savior of the world. (1st John 4:14)

Sheila Shelton

"But you, Bethlehem Ephrathah, though you are small among the clans of Judah, out of you will come for Me one who will be ruler over Israel, whose origins are of old, from ancient times." (Micah 5:2)

All inhabitants of the earth will worship the beast-all whose name have not been written in the Book of Life, belonging to the Lamb (Jesus) that was slain from the creation of the world. (Revelations 13:8)

For to us is born, to us a Son (Jesus) is given, and the government will be on His shoulders. And He will be called Wonderful Counselor, Mighty God, Everlasting Father, Prince of Peace. Of the increase of His government and peace, there will be no end. He will reign on David's throne and over His kingdom, establishing and upholding it with justice and righteousness from that time on and forever. The zeal of the Lord Almighty will accomplish this. (Isaiah 9:6, 7)

Dogs have surrounded Me (Jesus), a band of evil men has encircled Me, they have pierced My hands and My feet. (Psalm 22:16)

Surely He took up our infirmities and carried our sorrows, yet we considered Him (Jesus) stricken by God, smitten by Him, and afflicted. (Isaiah 53:4)

The Miracles In My Life

Now, brothers, I want to remind you of the gospel I preached to you, which you received and on which you have taken your stand. For what I received I passed on to you as of first importance; that Christ (Jesus) died for our sins according to Scripture, that He was buried, that He was raised on the third day according to the Scriptures. (1st Corinthians 15:1-4)

Beyond all questions, the mystery of godliness is great: He (Jesus) appeared in a body, was vindicated by the Spirit, was seen by angels, was preached among the nations, was believed on in the world, was taken up in glory. (1st Timothy 3:16)

Theirs are the patriarchs, and from them is traced the human ancestry of Christ, who is God over all, forever praised! Amen. (Romans 9:5)

"The Redeemer (Jesus) will come to Zion, to those in Jacob who repent of their sins," declares the Lord. (Isaiah 59:20)

I saw Heaven standing open and there before me was a white horse, whose rider is called Faithful and True. With justice He (Jesus) judges and makes war. The armies of Heaven were following Him (Jesus), riding on white horses and dressed in fine linen, white and clean. (Revelations 19:11, 14)

I have installed My King (Jesus) on Zion, My holy hill." (Psalm 2:6)

Because You (God) will not abandon Me to the grave, nor will You let Your holy One (Jesus) see decay. (Psalm 16:10)

I know that my Redeemer (Jesus) lives, and that in the end, He will stand upon the earth. And after My skin has been destroyed, yet in My flesh I will see God. (Job 19:25, 26)

Then, I heard what sounded like a great multitude, like the roar of rushing waters and like loud peals of thunder, shouting: "Hallelujah! For the Lord God Almighty reigns." (Revelations 19:6)

"He will be great and will be called the Son (Jesus) of the Most High. The Lord God will give Him the throne of His father David, and He will reign over the house of Jacob (Israel) forever; His kingdom will never end." (Luke 1:32, 33)

"Shout and be glad, O Daughter of Zion, for I (Jesus) am coming, and I will live among you" declares the Lord. (Zechariah 2:10)

After Jesus was born in Bethlehem in Judea, during the time of King Herod, Magi from the east came to Jerusalem, and asked, "Where is the One who has been born King of the Jews: We saw His

The Miracles In My Life

star in the east and have come to worship Him." (Matthew 2:1, 2)

"He (Jesus) will be great and will be called the Son of the Most High. The Lord God will give Him the throne of His father David, and He will reign over the house of Jacob forever; His kingdom will never end." (Luke 1:32, 33)

Who has gone up to Heaven (Jesus) and come down? Who has gathered up the wind in the hollow of His hands? Who has wrapped up the waters in His cloak? Who has established all the ends of the earth? What is His name, and the name of His Son? Tell me if you know! (Proverbs 30:4)

Pray for the peace of Jerusalem: "May those who love you be secure. (Psalm 122:6)

Then Jesus came to them and said, "All authority in Heaven and on earth has been given to Me. There, go and make disciples of all nations, baptizing them in the name of the Father, the Son (Jesus) and the Holy Spirit. (Matthew 28:18, 19)

There are sixty-six books in the Bible and sixty four were written by Jews. The two left, Luke and Acts were written by Luke, a Gentile.

The Bible was written by forty-four different men and took sixteen hundred years to write.

Sheila Shelton

The books of Daniel and Revelations were written six hundred fifty years apart, and talk about the beast with four heads, and it is symbolic, representing different countries.

The Lion is Great Britain, the Eagles' wings are the United States, the Bear is Russia and the Leopard represents Germany.

Chapter 16
Conclusion

There have been more personal things which have happened to me that I am hesitant to discuss, and have not added to his book.

I do know that the Holy Spirit talks to you, because I have experienced it.

When we pray, the Lord is always working even when we cannot see what he is doing, and we just have to wait patiently for His perfect timing. Otherwise, if we knew what He was doing, we might try to help and mess it up.

We all have a sinful nature, and were separated from God, and after salvation, we will get tempted to sin, but we have the Holy Spirit to help us in our weaknesses.

Jesus willingly took upon all our sins when He went to the cross, and all we have to do is believe in Him, and ask Him to forgive us of our sins and save our souls. It's that simple.

We are saved by believing in Jesus, and for turning from our sins.

No one has been so bad that Jesus won't save you, if you believe in Him.

The only person who has ever been perfect while on this earth is Jesus Himself. He was the perfect Lamb of God. If He had sinned while on this earth, He would not have qualified to die in our place. He had to be perfect.

After we are saved, God the Father looks on us and our sins are white as snow, because we are covered with Jesus' blood. His blood is powerful!

If we are reckless and do not change, then God's wrath will be upon us.

I still sin, because of my flesh, but I do not want to. I confess my sins daily to God the Father, in Jesus' name, and He forgives me. I have been forgiven. Praise God!

He who overcomes will, like them, be dressed in white. I will never blot out His name from the the Book of Life, but will acknowledge His name before My Father and His angels. (Revelations 3:5)

There is a void in everyone's life, an empty space that only the Lord Jesus can fill, and we will never be complete until we get saved and fill our lives with Him. It just gets better all the time! I promise.

Where will you choose to spend eternity? It's your choice.

The Poem

This is a poem that my precious sister, Lisa Windham wrote for me on September 16, 2000, and it means so much to me. I just had to add it.

My Sister, My Mother
I was living a life of sin and despair,
Not knowing our God, nor did I care.

The Miracles In My Life

But you dear sister would not leave me alone,
You explained it so boldly, over the phone.
You lead me to Christ, sweet sister of mind,
And you share in my joy, when I'm on cloud nine.
I know I'd be dead now, if not for you,
In hell there's no doubt, these words are true.
We're here for each other, through good times and bad,
Through sorrow and joy, happy and sad.
My Sister, My Mother, Sheila by name,
Oh how many victories are you going to claim?
In blood you're my sister, in Christ-my-mother
I could search the world, but like you there's no other.
We share a bond, that no one can break,
A love that's so special, it cannot be fake.
When we leave this world, I know in my heart,
That even in death we will not part.
So in Heaven I know that we'll see each other, and
It's all thanks to you, My Sister, My Mother.

(For Sheila, thanks for always being there for me! I love you bunches!!! God bless you!!!)

-Lisa Rhea Windham

Lisa has a talent for writing. God bless you, Lisa!

Chapter 17
Helpful Bible Verses

I will give You (Jesus) thanks in the great assembly; among throngs of people I will praise You. (Psalm 35:18)

Let the Word of Christ dwell in you richly as you teach and admonish one another with all wisdom, and as you sing psalms, hymns and spiritual songs with gratitude in your hearts to God. (Colossians 3:16)

In the same way, the Spirit helps us in our weakness. We do not know what we ought to pray for, but the Spirit Himself intercedes for us with groans that words cannot express. (Romans 8:26)

Sitting down, Jesus called the twelve and said, "If anyone wants to be first, he must be the very last, and the servant of all." (Mark 9:35)

Get rid of all bitterness, rage and anger, brawling and slander, along with every form of malice. Be kind and compassionate to one another, forgiving each other, just as in Christ, God forgave you. (Ephesians 4:31, 32)

And my God will meet all your needs according to His glorious riches in Christ Jesus. (Philippians 4:19)

And I (Jesus) will do whatever you ask in My name, so that the Son may bring glory to the Father. (John 14:13)

Commit thy way unto the Lord, trust also, in Him and He shall bring it to pass. (Psalm 37:5)

Seek His will in all you do, and He will show you which path to take. (Proverbs 3:6)

Are not two sparrows sold for a penny? Yet not one of them will fall to the ground apart from the will of your Father. (Mark 10:29)

I know that nothing good lives in me, that is, in my spiritual nature. For, I have the desire to do what is good, but I cannot carry it out. (Romans 7:18)

And I am certain that God, who began the good work within you, will continue His work until it is finally finished on the day when Jesus Christ returns. (Philippians 1:6)

Be joyful always; pray continually; give thanks in all circumstances, for this is God's will for you in Christ Jesus. (1st Thessalonians 5:16,17, 18)

Nothing is impossible to him who believes. (Mark 9:23)

I can do everything through Jesus who gives me strength. (Philippians 4:13)

But you are a chosen people, a royal priesthood, a holy nation a people belonging to God, that you may declare the praises of Him who called you out of darkness into his wonderful light. (1st Peter 2:9)

But the fruit of the Spirit is love, joy, peace, patience, kindness, goodness, faithfulness, gentleness and self-control. Against such there is no law. (Galatians 5:22,23)

Love is patient, love is kind, it does not envy, it does not boast, it is not proud. It is not rude, it is not self-seeking, it is not easily angered, it keeps no record of wrongs. Love does not delight in evil, but rejoices with the truth. It always protects, always trusts, always hopes, always perseveres. Love never fails…(1st Corinthians 13:4,5,6,7,8)

The tongue has the power of life and death, and those who love it will eat its fruit. (Proverbs 18:21)

Do not let this Book of the Law depart from your mouth; meditate on it day and night, so that you may be careful to do everything written in it. Then, you will be prosperous and successful. (Joshua 1:8)

To whom can I speak and give warning? Who will listen to me? Their ears are closed so they cannot hear. The word of the Lord is OFFENSIVE to them, they find no pleasure in it. (Jeremiah 6:10)

The fruit of the righteous is a tree of life, and he who wins souls is wise. (Proverbs 11:30)

Do not conform any longer to the pattern of the world, but be transformed by the renewing of your mind. Then you will be able to test and approve what God's will is-His good, pleasing and perfect will. (Romans 12:2)

And I want to show you great and marvelous things. (Jeremiah 33:3)

Commit to the Lord whatever you do, and your plans will succeed. (Proverbs 16:3)

Do not take revenge, my friends, but leave room for the Lord's wrath; for it is written: "It is mine to avenge; I will repay; says the Lord. (Romans 12:19)

Those who are wise will shine like the brightness of the heavens, and those who lead many to righteousness, like the stars forever and ever. (Daniel 12:3)

The Miracles In My Life

Many will be purified, made spotless and refined, but the wicked will continue to be wicked. None of the wicked will understand, but those who are wise will understand. (Daniel 12:10)

The Lord detests the way of the wicked, but he loves those who pursue righteousness. (Proverbs 15:9)

A hot-tempered man stirs up dissension, but a patient man calms a quarrel. (Proverbs 15:18)

I will tell the kindness of the Lord, the deeds for which He is to be praised, according to all the Lord has done for us- yes, the many good things He has done for the house of Israel, according to His compassion and many kindnesses. (Isaiah 63:7)

Tell everything. Hold on to the good. Avoid every kind of evil. (1st Thessalonians 5:21, 22)

Put God in remembrance of His promises, keep not silent. Give Him no rest until it comes to pass. (Isaiah 62:6, 7)

You are the God who performs miracles; you display Your power among the people. (Psalm 77:14)

Who then is the man that fears the Lord? He instructs him in the way chosen for him. (Psalm 25:12)

Sheila Shelton's facebook page is:

facebook.com/TheMiraclesInMyLife

sheila.shelton@hotmail.com